Romantic North Carolina

MORE THAN 300 THINGS TO DO
FOR SOUTHERN LOVERS

LISA M. DELLWO

JESSICA PHILYAW

d

HILL STREET PRESS   ATHENS, GEORGIA

A HILL STREET PRESS BOOK

Hill Street Press is committed to preserving the written word.
Every effort is made to print books on acid-free paper with a significant
amount of post-consumer recycled content.

Text and cover design by Anne Richmond Boston.

Printed in Canada.

Published in the United States of America by:

Hill Street Press LLC
191 East Broad Street, Suite 209
Athens, Georgia 30601-2848 USA
706-613-7200
info@hillstreetpress.com
www.hillstreetpress.com

Front cover postcard:
(*C. T. American Art Colored*) originally printed by Asheville Postcard Company.
Back cover postcard:
(*Genuine Curteich Chicago*) originally printed by Harry N. Martin.

2   4   6   8   10   9   7   5   3   1

ISBN # 1-892514-14-1

Library of Congress Cataloging-in-Publication Data

Dellwo, Lisa, 1959–
Romantic North Carolina : more than 300 things to do for southern lovers /
by Lisa Dellwo and Jessica Philyaw.
p.   cm.
ISBN 1-892514-14-1 (alk. paper)
1. North Carolina Guidebooks. 2. Couples—North Carolina.
I. Philyaw, Jessica, 1965– II. Title.
F252.3 .D45   1999
917.5604'43—dc21   99-34406
CIP

Contents

ACKNOWLEDGMENTS vii

INTRODUCTION ix

ARTS FOR THE HEART 1
Performance Venues 4
Theater 6
Dance 8
Musical Performances 9
A Night at the Movies 12
Starry-Eyed Love I 13
Museums 14
Museums on Campus 18
Starry-Eyed Love II 20

GET OUT OF THE HOUSE! 23
State and National Parks 26
Lakes 29
Other Scenic Destinations 32
Covered Bridges 33
Romantic Legends 33
Waterfalls 36
Lighthouses 38
Gold and Gem Mining 39
Alternative Forms of Transportation 41
Annual Sky Events 42
Spotlight: The Blue Ridge Parkway 43

PLAYING AROUND 47

Bicycling 50

Horseback Riding 52

Skiing 54

Boating 55

Scuba Diving and Snorkeling 58

Hang Gliding 59

Our Kind of Sport 60

LOVE IN THE BLEACHERS 61

College Sports 64

Minor League Baseball 66

Women's Softball and Soccer 67

Major League Pro Sports 68

Steeplechase 69

Celebrity Golf Tournaments 69

Spotlight: Get a Little Wild at the North Carolina Zoo 71

TAKE A WALK ON THE URBAN SIDE 73

Gallery Walks 75

Shopping and Downtown Strolling 79

Gardens 82

Cemeteries 87

FEEDING YOUR LOVE 89

Dinner Out 92

Meals on Wheels—or Water 95

Picnic Purveyors 97

Specialty Foods 98

A Jug of Wine . . . 100

Winetasting Classes 103

The Couple That Cooks Together . . . 104

Food Festivals 107

Spotlight: Fall in Love at the State Fair 109

A NIGHT ON THE TOWN 111
  Lucky in Love 113
  Comedy Clubs 114
  Do You Want to Dance? 115
  A Literary Night Out 117
  Getting There in Style 119

LET'S SPEND THE NIGHT TOGETHER 123
  One of a Kind 125
  Country Inns and Bed and Breakfasts 126
  Upscale Lodging 132
  Resorts for Sports 134

APPENDIX: FURTHER RESOURCES 137

INDEX 141

To Bill and Scott,
who make North Carolina that much more romantic

Acknowledgements Our work was made easier

because of the suggestions made by many friends, their friends, colleagues, and others.

These friends, old and new, provided valuable suggestions and feedback: Catherine W. Bishir, Michael McFee, Kathy Ketterman, Johanna Grimes, David Perry, Annette Windhorn, Ann Windhorn, Candace Bruce, Mary Putman, Claire Kirch and Joel Sipress, Maureen Ahmad and Jim Crawford, Bernice Bergup, Anne Vilen and Bill Kwochka, Michael and Barbara Hudson, Joyce Moore, June and Newton Smith, Laura Wenzel, Steve Brumfield, Tricia Bowers Hudson, Laura Poole, Lee Willoughby-Harris, Jane Sears Thompson, Jack Claiborne, Sally McMillan, Eddie Nickens, Jeannie Saunders, Jan Schochet, Mark Walbridge and Ann Bartuska, Jim Clark and Chantal Reid, Richard and Beth Thomas, and Jim and Mary Siedow (whose suggestion, unfortunately, we couldn't use, because this isn't that sort of book).

Although it was their job to be helpful to us, these people, either tourism professionals or associated with organizations mentioned, went beyond the call of duty to provide information: Buck Rogers, Adriene Heffner, Mary Beth Lackey, Bill Graham, Julie L. Smith, Ed Kaminski, Martin Armes, Jackie Harvey, Bob Kopetsky, Tania Dautlick, Jenny Lobdell, Michael S. Pleasant, Rick

Coley, Bill Arnold, Eden Foster, Ed Purdy, Jessica Wucki, Connie Nelson, and Pamela Thibodeau.

We thank Tom Payton and the other folks at Hill Street Press for entrusting us with this thoroughly enjoyable project. Our husbands, Bill and Scott, provided creative ideas and critical readings of the manuscript. We thank them, and Adam and David, for love, support, and (in Jessica's case) computer time.

If it is your time, love will track you down like a cruise missile.—Lynda Barry

Introduction No matter what you've heard about our northern neighbor, North Carolina is truly for lovers. With miles of white sand beaches to the east and stately mountains to the west, our state's scenic beauty alone makes it a perfect setting for romance. Our cities, with lively shopping districts and world-class museums, performing arts centers, and sports teams, are bursting with dating destinations. And our countryside offers wineries to tour, lakes and rivers to paddle, and peaceful country inns for a refreshing break from the routine.

Whether you're planning your first date or your second honeymoon, this book is for you. We've also included outings for every budget and just about every age group. Most of the dates and destinations we describe are great for out-of-state visitors, but a handful of them (such as cooking classes) are more suitable for residents.

While we've included well more than the 300 romantic adventures promised in the subtitle, we have had to omit hundreds of others in order to keep the book to a manageable size. *Romantic North Carolina* is intended as an idea book, suggesting the wealth of possibilities North Carolina offers to lovers. We haven't listed every picnic basket purveyor, symphony orchestra, or scenic overlook, but we hope these entries will inspire you to craft your own romantic outing.

WHO WE ARE

Because you'll encounter us periodically throughout the book, introductions are in order. Lisa lives with her husband Bill in an urban area of central North Carolina and Jessica with her husband Scott and their two sons in a small college town in the mountains. You'll find Lisa and Bill's influence in the sections on driving trips, gallery walks, and winery tours, and Jessica and Scott's in the descriptions of hiking and picnics. For better or for worse, all of us influenced the food-related entries. Because of the harried pace of both households, you'll find a lot of entries in the book that offer privacy, or what Lisa calls "face time": nature walks, scenic drives, even cemetery strolls!

To keep the book from reflecting just our interests, we called on many friends and colleagues for ideas. Many of them forwarded our request to their own friends and colleagues, resulting in a gratifying number of calls, emails, and letters from complete strangers who wanted to help us define romantic North Carolina. They are properly thanked in the Acknowledgements.

Both of us are long-time transplants to North Carolina, and although we'd gotten to know our adopted state pretty well, one of the pleasures of researching this book was the many new discoveries we made, including llama treks, the state's wineries, and its many botanical gardens.

WHAT IS ROMANTIC, ANYWAY?

In a book whose entries range from sunset strolls to professional hockey, how do we define romantic, and where do we set the limits? As you'll see, we've kept the concept of romance fairly elastic, and the suggestions we received from our informants kept our own ideas from predominating.

So what's romantic? Just about anything, provided both members of the couple are interested. We don't want to hear about anyone being forced to go to the ballet or to a Panthers game because "it's in the book." Look for outings here that will reflect a shared love (of nature, sports, and food) or in which you can introduce your date to a longtime passion that you hope to share in the future. Above all, have fun!

How to Use This Book

This guidebook is organized thematically, so that nature lovers can find all sorts of suggestions in one chapter, sports fans in another, fine arts aficionados in another, and so on. If you're trying to plan an outing in a particular city or locate a specific site, we suggest that you consult the comprehensive index.

As we organized our material, we discovered a handful of special attractions—like the State Fair and the North Carolina Zoo—that wouldn't fit within the confines of one particular chapter. So you'll find three "Spotlights" interwoven between the chapters. Each chapter also includes several sidebars that are related to its subject matter.

To assist those who live in—or are planning to travel to—a particular region, we've devised geographic codes that accompany each entry. Following the lead of the North Carolina Division of Tourism, Film and Sports Development, we've divided the state into three regions:

 = **The Coast: approximately east of Interstate 95**

 = **The Mountains: approximately west of Interstate 77**

 = **The Heartland: also known as the Piedmont**

Because the heartland is the largest section geographically and encompasses most of the state's large urban areas, you'll find more entries from that region than from the two others.

Each entry includes address and phone information and a web-site address when available. In some cases—such as state parks or lakes—we have omitted street addresses for obvious reasons. We have also left them out when we felt they might be confusing; for instance the North Carolina Symphony, which has a Raleigh office address, performs in many different localities; your best bet is to call the box office number we have listed for information or to consult the website. In a few instances, particularly when discussing gallery or shopping districts, no phone number is included.

ROMANTIC NORTH CAROLINA HALL OF FAME

Even as we were researching this book, people began asking us for advice on romantic outings. So we present here the "Romantic North Carolina Hall of Fame"—ten memorable dates that you'll find described in detail in the book. We hope you'll find a winner in this list:

- ♥ *Spend the night in North Carolina's only Boat and Breakfast, operated by Winds of Carolina Sailing Tours in Southport.*
- ♥ *Tour the award-winning (and beautiful) Westbend Winery, outside of Winston-Salem.*
- ♥ *Take a ride and enjoy a meal on the Twilight Dinner Train, embarking in Dillsboro.*
- ♥ *Take a moonlight "wafting" trip down the Eno River in Durham; everyone looks beautiful in moonlight!*
- ♥ *Bring a picnic to an outdoor music performance or movie screening at the North Carolina Museum of Art in Raleigh.*

♥ *Ride a rented tandem bike along the bicycle trails of the Outer Banks.*

♥ *Explore the arts district of historic north Charlotte in the twice-monthly Davidson Gallery Crawl.*

♥ *Discover "Kindred Spirits" in a solitary stretch of Sunset Beach.*

♥ *Learn to dance the Argentine Tango—a two-and-a-half minute love affair—at Roland's Dance Studio in Fayetteville.*

♥ *Get hitched at the Grove Park Inn in Asheville; they'll provide the magistrate, witnesses, bridal bouquet, and wedding cake for two!*

HAVE WE LEFT OUT YOUR FAVORITE ROMANTIC THING TO DO IN NORTH CAROLINA?

As we mentioned earlier, this book is intended to be an idea book, not an encyclopedic reference. In our appendix, you'll find a list of resources to help you research your own romatic outing, including organizations, publications, and websites.

If you'd like us to consider adding your favorite romantic destination to a future edition, please write us:

Romantic North Carolina
c/o Hill Street Press
191 East Broad Street, Suite 209
Athens, GA 30601-2848

Arts
for the
Heart

*It was a love like a chord from Bach
of such pure gravity.*—Nina Cassian

Imagine this: you and your date dress up in black tie and attend a Broadway production, the ballet, or the symphony. Or instead, take in the premieres of potentially award-winning films at a prestigious film festival. Or play hooky from work and spend an afternoon exploring the exhibits at a world-class museum. You're probably thinking, "Sounds great. But I don't have the time or money to spend a week in New York or Washington."

News flash—you don't have to travel to the big city to enjoy a show, see a film festival, or go to a great museum. North Carolina is filled with opportunities to take in the arts. In addition to highlighting our great performing arts centers and museums, in this chapter we also remind you of smaller, unusual, and even offbeat places that you'll find only in North Carolina. And we invite you to take your date to a planetarium (hint: it's dark!) or one of the few drive-in movie theaters that hasn't been converted to a flea market. We also list annual music festivals whose offerings range from bluegrass to jazz to classical. And we wind up the chapter with three outstanding ways to share an evening under the real stars, listening to music or seeing a film and enjoying a picnic dinner together.

First, an apology. No matter where you live in North Carolina, you'll be surprised at how close you are to a municipal symphony, chorale, theater, ballet, or opera company. We are proud of and even overwhelmed by the number of local troupes we discovered, and space simply doesn't permit our listing them all. So our focus here is on the statewide companies, with this additional advice: check your yellow pages or local arts weekly for much, much more. Now, on with the show!

PERFORMANCE VENUES

From the coast to the mountains, you can enjoy an evening of music, dance, or theater at a number of performance venues that book nationally touring acts. These halls range from the large and elegant to the small and intimate, and they are all classy places to bring your sweetheart.

The North Carolina Blumenthal Performing Arts Center in the heart of Charlotte is so glamorous that you'll want to dress to the nines and enjoy a pre-theater dinner for a memorable date. The Broadway Lights series brings in top-notch touring Broadway productions, including, recently, *Bring in 'Da Noise/Bring in 'Da Funk* and *Rent*, and it has also hosted performances by Riverdance, Wynton Marsalis, and Patty Loveless. In addition, the Charlotte Symphony Orchestra and the North Carolina Dance Company call the Blumenthal Center home.

North Carolina Blumenthal Performing Arts Center
130 North Tryon Street / Charlotte / 704-372-1000
www.performingartsctr.com

Equally elegant but with a much more storied history is Wilmington's Thalian Hall. Built in 1858 and restored after a fire in the 1970s, this large theater is a major stop for touring artists and performing arts companies, including, for instance, the Paul

Taylor Dance Company, Ronnie Milsap, and Le Trio Gershwin of Paris.

Thalian Hall Center for the Performing Arts
310 Chestnut Street / Wilmington / 910-343-3664
or 800-523-2820

The Earl Wynn Theater at the ArtsCenter in Carrboro is a more intimate and informal setting if you're not into sequins and tuxedoes. Although there are some theatrical programs here, the ArtsCenter is known for attracting national jazz acts like the Charles McPherson Quartet. Other musical acts that pass through the Earl Wynn Theater include the Rev. Billy Wirtz (not to be missed if you can take your music with a wild sense of humor) and the Red Clay Ramblers, North Carolina's internationally known string band.

Earl Wynn Theater
ArtsCenter / 300-G West Main Street / Carrboro
919-929-2787 / mcdwebdesign.com/artscenter

In Winston-Salem, the North Carolina School of the Arts is a unique state-supported school devoted to training students in dance, filmmaking, drama, music, and the visual arts. As part of its mission the school hosts performances by internationally known acts in all of these fields, including recently, the Mendelssohn String Quartet, the Vienna Boys Choir, and a stage adaptation of Dickens's Little Dorrit.

North Carolina School of the Arts
533 South Main Street / Winston-Salem / 336-721-1945
www.ncarts.edu

Even North Carolina's traditional colleges and universities get in on the act. As you'll find throughout this guide, we think their campuses offer great resources for the romantically inclined. Many of them offer performing arts series that bring in the same quality of major touring shows as the other venues we've mentioned. We've listed just a few here, but call your nearby college or university for other possibilities.

Mainstage Series
Appalachian State University / Boone / 800-841-ARTS (2787)

Carolina Union Performing Arts Series
University of North Carolina at Chapel Hill / 919-962-1449

Professional Performing Arts Series
North Carolina State University / Raleigh / 919-515-1100

Davidson College Artists Series
Davidson College / Davidson / 704-892-2135

Broadway at Duke, Duke University Institute of the Arts, Duke
Artists Series, Chamber Arts Society
Durham / 919-684-4444

S. Rudolph Alexander Performing Arts Series
East Carolina University / Greenville
252-328-4788 or 800-ECU-ARTS (328-2787)

THEATER

Although all of the performance venues listed above host theatrical productions, we wanted to let you know about a few that specialize in them. Whether you're into comedy, tragedy, farce, or (of course) a good love story, you'll find some magic together at the theater.

Flat Rock has been a popular vacation destination for a century, and poet Carl Sandburg even built a house nearby. For modern romantics, there's the Flat Rock Playhouse, also called the State

Theatre of North Carolina. Every year from May to October, the Vagabond Players put on comedies, musicals, farces, and who-dunits of such quality that it is considered one of the ten best seasonal theaters in the country.

Flat Rock Playhouse
2661 Greenville Highway / Flat Rock / 828-693-0731

We are really impressed with Duke University's commitment to the performing arts. In addition to the series listed in the previous section, Duke has recently launched Theater Previews, in which a show bound for a national stage has its first performances at Duke's Reynolds Industries Theater. The first two shows, *Kudzu: A Southern Musical* and *Eleanor: An American Love Story* subsequently had runs at Ford's Theatre in Washington.

Theater Previews
Duke University / Durham / 919-684-4444 or 800-955-5566

Few playwrights penned love stories with the style and substance of Shakespeare. Well before Shakespeare was in love in the movies, the annual North Carolina Shakespeare Festival, held in High Point, was popularizing the playwright's work. From August to October, the Festival produces masterworks of classic theater with a focus, of course, on the Bard.

North Carolina Shakespeare Festival
High Point / 336-841-2273

In nearby Winston-Salem, the National Black Theatre Festival is an exciting celebration of black theater and performers. For a week every August, artists like Harry Belafonte, Debbie Allen, Sidney Poitier, Della Reese, and John Amos grace the stages of this

Piedmont city. In addition, the North Carolina Black Repertory Company calls Winston-Salem home.

> **National Black Theatre Festival and North Carolina Black Repertory Company**
> **610 Coliseum Drive / Winston-Salem / 336-723-7907**

DANCE

If you love modern dance, you probably already know that North Carolina is home to the American Dance Festival, which has become one of the most prestigious international dance events. Every year for six weeks, the likes of the Merce Cunningham Dance Company, Pilobolus Dance Theatre, and the Paul Taylor Dance Company perform for more than 32,000 people in Duke University's Page Auditorium and Reynolds Industries Theater. Many works have premiered at the Festival, including some commissioned for the festival or by individuals. (Now that would be a great way to impress your date!)

> **American Dance Festival**
> **Durham / 919-684-6402 / www.AmericanDanceFestival.org**

The recently formed Carolina Ballet performs classics like Prokofief's *Romeo and Juliet* as well as more innovative offerings. In its inaugural 1999 season, it also paired with Duke University's renowned Ciompi Quartet for a trio of world premiere "Chamber Ballets" performed, of course, to live chamber music.

> **Carolina Ballet**
> **Raleigh / 919-303-6303 / www.carolinaballet.com**

MUSICAL PERFORMANCES

Music is the expression of harmony in sound. Love is the expression of harmony in life.—*Stephen F. Gaskin*

Whether you like chamber music or shape-note singing (or both), North Carolina has plenty to offer lovers who are music lovers. In addition to organizations that perform year-round, the state is particularly rich in annual music festivals that attract renowned performers.

A night at the symphony is a superb way to share your love of music. Since 1932, the North Carolina Symphony has entertained and educated audiences with classical and pops concerts. Based at Raleigh's Memorial Auditorium, the Symphony performs concerts throughout the state, and it hosts world-class guest musicians like Nadja Salerno-Sonnenberg. If your passion for music is rich, but you're broke, you can take a date to one of the symphony's Open Rehearsals. And for those still searching for their true love, the Symphony Singles meets for meals on Saturday nights before concerts. Later in this chapter, you'll find more about the Symphony's summer outdoor performances.

North Carolina Symphony
Raleigh / 919-733-2750 / www.ncsymphony.org

The Eastern Music Festival, which takes place for six weeks every summer at Greensboro's Guilford College, is a superb educational opportunity for talented student musicians with a bonus for music lovers: there are public performances almost every night by advanced students and high-caliber guest artists.

Eastern Music Festival
Greensboro / 336-333-7450 / www.easternmusicfestival.com

The Blue Ridge Mountains provide an appropriately dramatic backdrop for the annual Brevard Music Festival. Every summer instructors and guest performers at the Brevard Music School fill the mountains with the sounds of symphonic, show, chamber, pops, and opera music. Guest performers ranging from Frederica von Stade and Van Cliburn to Marvin Hamlisch and Tony Bennett have contributed to the renown of this venerable festival.

Brevard Music Festival
Brevard / 828-884-2011 / www.brevardmusic.org

On a cool February weekend in Wilmington, national jazz and Dixieland acts heat things up during the North Carolina Jazz Festival. Get your tickets well in advance, because the shows sell out early. After a Thursday night preview at Thalian Hall, the Festival moves to the more intimate ballroom of the Hilton Wilmington Riverside.

North Carolina Jazz Festival
Wilmington / 910-343-3664 or 800-523-2820

Every September, the old Durham Athletic Park, immortalized in the movie *Bull Durham*, hosts the Bull Durham Blues Festival. Blues-loving visitors from all over the country arrive in Durham—birthplace of the Piedmont Blues-to hear the likes of Lightnin' Wells, Wilson Pickett, and up-and-coming blues guitarist Deborah Coleman. Sponsored by the St. Joseph's Historic Foundation.

Bull Durham Blues Festival
Durham Athletic Park / 428 Morris Street / Durham
919-683-1709

On almost any balmy weekend in North Carolina, you could take a date to a festival celebrating traditional and folk music, especially in the mountain region. Our sentimental favorite is MerleFest, honoring the music of the late Merle Watson and his well-known father, Doc Watson, because Lisa saw Merle and Doc perform together less than a year before Merle's untimely death. (They were great!) Bluegrass, jazz, folk, contemporary, and Cajun music are played side-by-side over the course of one busy weekend every April.

🌲 **MerleFest**
Wilkesboro / 336-838-6267 or 800-343-7857
www.merlefest.org

A terrific way to share a musical evening with your date is the Songwriters in the Round program hosted approximately once a month at the Balsam Mountain Inn. Four or more award-winning songwriters are invited to the elegant dining room to perform together while you dine. Sitting in a circle facing each other, they perform their signature songs (often made famous by other vocalists) and just jam together. While most of the songwriters are from the country and bluegrass tradition, jazz and pop writers are sometimes part of the show. The informality of the evening lends itself to a lot of fun and interaction with the audience, but the meal you are served is elegant indeed. Your table is yours for the entire evening, and you may be seated at any time you wish, before or during the performance.

🌲 **Songwriters in the Round**
Balsam Mountain Inn / US Highway 23/74
Balsam / 828-456-9498 or 800-224-9498
www.aksi.net/~cmark/balsam.htm

A NIGHT AT THE MOVIES

Going to the movies is the classic date, and for very good reason. For first dates, you can get through that awkward, getting-to-know-you stage by spending a few hours focusing on the movie and then sharing your thoughts on it afterwards. And on subsequent dates, depending on how the relationship is going, a few hours together in the dark is either (a) a lot of fun or (b) an excuse for not having to talk to your date. We don't think you need any help finding the nearest Cine-Multi-Plex, but we do have some suggestions for more offbeat movie outings.

Once upon a time, you could take your date to a drive-in movie and probably run into all the other kids from the high school. Most of these theaters are now defunct, but if you can find one still in operation, it'll be a fun, nostalgic evening. And hey, if you want to hop into the back seat, we won't tell. These drive-ins show classic or first-run movies in the PG to R arena.

Belmont Drive-In Theatre
314 McAdenville Road / Belmont
704-825-6044

Bright Leaf Drive In Theatre
US Highway 52 North / Mount Airy
336-786-5494

Raleigh Road Outdoor Theatre
Raleigh Road / Henderson
919-438-6957

Made in North Carolina
A Trio of
Home-Grown Films

Since 1985, North Carolina has been one of the hottest film-making states, ranking third after California and New York most years. The moderate climate, varied landscape, and effective efforts of the North Carolina Film Office have all contributed to our success in getting filmmakers on location here, along with stars like Whoopi Goldberg, Tommy Lee Jones, Danny Glover, Harrison Ford, Tom Cruise, and Laura Dern. Hits including The Fugitive, Being There, The Color Purple, The Hunt for Red October, Days of Thunder, *and* Blue Velvet *were filmed partly or wholly in North Carolina.*

🌲 **Waynesville Drive In Theatre**
1823 Asheville Road / Waynesville
828-456-3562

For a slightly more sophisticated movie outing, two film festivals offer the opportunity to see classic or world premiere films. Wilmington is the moviemaking capital of the state (see sidebar) and host of the Cucalorus Film Festival, allowing North Carolina filmmakers to share their talent with their peers and the public. In Durham, the DoubleTake Documentary Film Festival, still in its infancy, boasts a board including Martin Scorsese and Patricia Neal and has premiered films by Ken Burns and others. Both festivals take place in April.

🎬 **Cucalorus Film Festival**
Wilmington / 910-343-3664 or
910-815-6757 / www.cucalorus.org

🏢 **DoubleTake Documentary Film Festival**
Durham / 919-660-3699
www.doubletakemagazine.org/filmfestival

STARRY-EYED LOVE I

We were surprised at the number of people who suggested a visit to a planetarium as a romantic adventure, but think about it:

If you're looking for a good love story made in North Carolina, here are a few favorites:

Dirty Dancing

Jennifer Grey and Patrick Swayze portray lovers from the wrong side of the tracks who meet up and fall in love on the dance floor of a Catskills resort. Much of the movie was filmed on and around beautiful Lake Lure.

Last of the Mohicans

The Blue Ridge Mountains near Asheville portray the Leatherstocking Country of James Fenimore Cooper's novel, and Daniel Day-Lewis and Madeleine Stowe star in yet another tale of star-crossed love.

Bull Durham

We love Bull Durham *because not only was it filmed in North Carolina, it was also set here. Kevin Costner, Susan Sarandon, and Tim Robbins made the Durham Bulls the most recognized minor league team in the country in this romantic comedy.*

planetariums provide the all the allure of stargazing on a summer night without the mosquitoes! Snuggle up in the dark with your sweetheart and contemplate eternal love. Be aware that planetariums are also popular destinations for grade school groups, so choose an evening program for peaceful planetary contemplation.

Morehead Planetarium
East Franklin Street (UNC Campus) / Chapel Hill
919-962-1236 / www.morehead.unc.edu

Elizabeth City State University Planetarium
1704 Weeksville Road / Elizabeth City / 919-335-3SKY (3759)

MUSEUMS

Art is the accomplice of love.—Jane Stanton

North Carolina boasts a handful of world-class museums and some that are in a class all their own. A trip to a museum is a great way to while away a rainy weekend afternoon, but in order to enjoy the collection—and the companionship of your date—we say play hooky from work or school and enjoy a leisurely stroll through the collections of one or more of these museums. Be aware that many are closed on Mondays and some charge admission fees.

The North Carolina Museum of Art is a great romantic destination. The collection is outstanding, with Greek and Roman sculpture, European paintings and sculpture from the Renaissance through the Impressionist period, works of modern art by artists like Georgia O'Keeffe and Marsden Hartley, and a fine collection of Jewish ceremonial art. The romantically inclined should look for the first-century Roman statue of Aphrodite, goddess of love and beauty, or Elizabeth Louise Vigee Le Brun's painting of Count Ivan Ivanovitch Shuvalov, who gloried in the title of "Gentleman of the

Imperial Bedchamber" in the court of Empress Elisabeth I of Russia. Be sure to stop for a cappuccino or lunch at the Museum Café.

North Carolina Museum of Art
2110 Blue Ridge Road / Raleigh / 919-833-1935
www2.ncsu.edu/NCMA

Before the North Carolina Museum of Art, there was the Mint Museum—North Carolina's first art museum. Housed in a building that was once home to the first branch of the U.S. Mint, the Mint's permanent collections focus on European paintings, furniture, crafts, and decorative arts—including an important collection of pottery and porcelain. The new Mint Museum of Craft + Design extends the Mint's focus on ceramics and includes exhibits of glass, fiber, metal, and wood.

The Mint Museum of Art
2730 Randolph Road / Charlotte / 704-337-2000
www.mintmuseum.org

Mint Museum of Craft + Design
220 North Tryon Street / Charlotte, 704-337-2000

Reynolda House was built in 1912–1917 as part of the thousand-acre estate of Katharine Smith and tobacco magnate Richard Joshua Reynolds. You can still see original furnishings lovingly chosen for their home along with first-rate examples of American art, including paintings by Mary Cassatt and Thomas Eakins and prints by Jasper Johns. The costume collection includes Katharine's handsewn wedding dress. After you've seen the artwork, take a stroll through nearby Reynolda Gardens (April is cherry blossom season) and the shops and restaurants of Reynolda Village.

Reynolda House Museum of American Art
Reynolda Road / Winston-Salem / 336-725-5325
www.reynoldahouse.org

If your true love is a history buff, don't miss Tryon Palace. Back when North Carolina was a colony and New Bern was its capital, a beautiful Georgian house was built for Royal Governor William Tryon; subsequently it was the capitol of the independent state of North Carolina. The palace complex actually includes three restored historic homes with differing architectural styles, and costumed interpreters provide tours and history lessons.

Tryon Palace Historic Sites and Gardens
Pollock and George Streets / New Bern
252-514-4900 or 800-767-1560 / www.tryonpalace.org

The Whalehead Club in Corolla is a museum we like as much for its romantic history as for its mission. During a time when hunt clubs proliferated on the Outer Banks, Amanda Knight was refused admission to any of them because, even though she was an avid hunter, she was a woman. So she and her husband, Edward, built their own, complete with a cork dance floor and Art Nouveau trimmings, including fixtures by Tiffany. The Whalehead is being renovated and will eventually be a wildlife museum, but in the meantime visitors can tour this monument to the Knights' devotion.

Whalehead Club
NC Highway 12 / Corolla / 252-453-4343 (ext. 37)

If visiting other people's homes puts you in the mood to furnish your own, take an excursion to Seagrove and the North Carolina Pottery Center. There you'll find examples of work by the state's famous folk potters, some of whom are still working nearby. Once you've decided what you like, pick up a map and visit some of Seagrove's working potteries to purchase your own future antique.

North Carolina Pottery Center
250 East Avenue / Seagrove / 336-873-8430
www.ncpotterycenter.com

A romantic story is also behind one of the state's best-publicized museums. When Tom Banks was a twelve-year-old schoolboy in eastern North Carolina, he had a crush on a secretarial student he saw every day after school. Noticing his attention, one day she chased him down and gave him a playful kiss. A few years later he saw the object of his youthful desire in a newspaper and learned her name for the first time—Ava Gardner. Over the years, Banks and his wife collected every bit of Ava memorabilia they could find, and this collection forms the basis of the Ava Gardner Museum in Smithfield. At the museum, true devotees can pick up a map to Ava's birthplace and burial site, both nearby. To keep the Ava theme going, the folks at the museum suggest getting your hands on a video of *One Touch of Venus*, one of the most traditional love stories Gardner filmed.

Ava Gardner Museum
205 South Third Street / Smithfield / 919-934-5830
www.avagardner.org

Finally, we don't necessarily find visits to a natural science museum romantic (it's something about all those prehistoric skeletons). But we *love* "Love in the Tropics," the annual fundraiser sponsored by the Friends of the North Carolina Museum of Natural Sciences on or near Valentine's Day. There's dancing to a live band, food, and a cash bar, as well as a silent auction in which you might score yet another romantic outing, such as dinner at a local restaurant or an overnight stay in a nearby bed and breakfast. Scattered around on cards you'll find "Love Bites"—factoids about animal love. For instance, adult love bugs, who live only three to five days, may spend half of their brief lives, well, fooling around. In the breeding season, male geckos grab the first lizard in reach. If it's another male, a fight ensues. You may prefer the parrot, the most committed of birds—many mate for life.

🏠 **Love in the Tropics**
North Carolina Museum of Natural Sciences
Bicentennial Plaza / Raleigh / 919-733-7450
www.naturalsciences.org

MUSEUMS ON CAMPUS

Throughout this book we highlight the romantic possibilities offered by colleges and universities, from performance venues to botanical gardens. We were especially astonished at the number of museums on our state's campuses. If you work or live on campus, sneak away with your lover for an afternoon browsing one of these collections. Even if you're not associated with a university, these are worth a visit-just try summer, spring, or fall break to avoid parking pitfalls.

Exhibits focus on North Carolina folk art, western paintings and sculpture from the Middle Ages, Greek and Roman art:

🏠 **Ackland Art Museum**
University of North Carolina at Chapel Hill
South Columbia Street at Franklin Street / Chapel Hill
919-966-5736

Exhibits focus on the history and culture of Southern Appalachia:

🌲 **Appalachian Cultural Museum**
Appalachian State University / University Hall Drive
Boone / 828-262-3117

Exhibitions of artwork reflecting African American heritage:

🏠 **Diggs Gallery**
Winston-Salem State University
601 South Martin Luther King Jr. Drive / Winston-Salem
336-750-2458

Especially notable are the pre-Columbian collection and the Brummer collection of medieval and renaissance art:

Duke University Museum of Art
Campus Drive (east campus) / Durham / 919-684-5135

One of the nation's largest collections of African art and artifacts:

Mattye Reed African Heritage Center
North Carolina A&T University / 1601 East Market Street
Greensboro / 336-334-7874

Exhibits focus on Southern Appalachian history and culture:

Mountain Heritage Center
Western Carolina University
Robinson Administration Building / Cullowhee / 828-227-7129

Exhibits about the peoples and cultures of Africa, Asia, Oceana, and the Americas:

Museum of Anthropology
Wake Forest University / Wingate Road / Winston-Salem
336-758-5282

Exhibits of arts and crafts depicting tribal Indian life:

Native American Resource Center
University of North Carolina at Pembroke
Old Main Building / Lumberton / 910-521-6282

Contemporary art collections featuring prints and bronzes by Henri Matisse:

Weatherspoon Art Gallery
University of North Carolina at Greensboro
Spring Garden and Tate Streets / 336-445-5770

STARRY-EYED LOVE II

We've already introduced you to the romantic possibilities of planetariums. There's another way to share love under the stars, and it's one of our favorites, even if the bugs are biting. Here are three opportunities to enjoy a film, a musical performance, or both under the summer sky. Arrive with your picnic dinner before the program begins (don't forget the corkscrew!). Then as dusk arrives, settle back for an evening of entertainment.

Every summer, the North Carolina Museum of Art hosts a series of outdoor films and musical performances at its Joseph M. Bryan, Jr., Theater and Outdoor Cinema. Go early to stake out a prime bit of lawn, and bring a picnic. We've seen elaborate candlelit dinners with wine served in crystal goblets. You can also reserve a picnic dinner to be picked up when you arrive. The films tend to be arty, and the music eclectic.

North Carolina Museum of Art
2110 Blue Ridge Road / Raleigh / 919-839-6262
www2.ncsu.edu/NCMA

In a similar vein, Charlotte's Mint Museum sponsors the Jazzy Ladies series every summer. Your evening on the Mint's lawn begins with live entertainment by a local jazz vocalist-thus the "Jazzy Ladies" moniker. Then when it's sufficiently dark, you're treated to a movie. Each year's film series has a special focus, from musicals to monster movies.

Jazzy Ladies
Mint Museum / 2730 Randolph Road / Charlotte
704-337-2000

Every year from late May to July 4, the North Carolina Symphony goes outdoors for Summerfest, a series of performances held in Cary's Regency Park. Saturday nights are devoted to pops concerts, usually with guest performers. On several Thursdays the Symphony offers "Classical Twilight Zone," featuring light classical music, often with some explanations by the conductor. (Call it Symphony 101.) The gates open at 5:00 for the 7:30 concert, so you can enjoy your picnic dinner (catered meals are offered) and take a stroll on the park's walking trail before settling down to the music. The season concludes with a free July 4TH pops concert, and while the price is right, this popular event is really too crowded for a truly romantic evening. Take in one of the May or June concerts for cooler and quieter ambiance.

Summerfest
North Carolina Symphony / Regency Park / Cary
919-733-2750

Get Out
of the
House!

Love is a canvas furnished by nature and embroidered by imagination.—Voltaire

Getting out in nature with your sweetheart is a terrific way to kindle (or rekindle) romance in your relationship, and North Carolina has some of the best nature around—from the peaks of the Great Smoky Mountains to the white sands of the Outer Banks. With a full tank of gas, you can get to all parts in between in less than a day.

In this chapter, we start by highlighting a few of the outstanding national and state parks located in North Carolina. These can provide anything from a few hours to several days of quality time with your companion. Next, we highlight a few of the state's many recreational lakes, which offer boating, swimming, fishing, and, of course, sunbathing. For scenic places with a bit of history, we'll direct you to the only two covered bridges in the state, where you can find just enough privacy to steal a kiss. And if you're a sucker for a good love story, we'll show you where to find the scenic areas that have romantic legends associated with them.

Want your love to reach new heights? Cast your eye skyward toward some of the state's mountain waterfalls, or visit the coast's towering lighthouses. On a different tack, we suggest a little bit of old-fashioned silliness, courtesy of Mother Nature's natural resources: do-it-yourself gold and gem mining. We'll tell you where to go to find a little something that sparkles. Last, we bring you some amusing alternative forms of transportation in the great outdoors and a couple of annual events that should get your relationship of the ground.

STATE AND NATIONAL PARKS

All of the following parks offer camping, hiking, and enough outdoor activities to keep you coming back for more. You can plan a romantic getaway lasting a couple of days or up to a week (or even longer) to any of these wilderness areas. And depending on where you are traveling from, a day trip might be just what you want. Of necessity, this list is only a sampling of North Carolina's many state and national parks. For a complete list of parks, we suggest that you visit your local bookstore or library to take a look some of the many comprehensive outdoor guides to the state. You can also contact:

North Carolina Division of Parks and Recreation
Raleigh / 919-733-PARK (7275)
www.ils.unc.edu/parkproject/ncparks.html

National Park Service
www.nps.gov

The Blue Ridge Mountains and the Great Smoky Mountains make the western part of the state a special destination for folks from around the world just as it is for Tar Heel natives. Indeed, the Great Smoky Mountains National Park, which straddles the North Carolina–Tennessee border, is the most visited national park in the country. (And the crowds aren't nearly as bad as at Yosemite.) Despite the large number of visitors who come each year, the park's primary romantic attractions are the innumerable easily accessed trails that provide calm, beauty, and solitude. Whether on an extended back country hike or picnicking a mile from the parking lot, you and your loved one can readily find enough privacy to imagine yourselves to be truly alone in the wilderness. For rugged mountain beauty east of the Mississippi, it just doesn't get any better than the Smokies.

 **Great Smoky Mountains
National Park
Cherokee and Bryson City
615-436-1230**

Joyce Kilmer Memorial Forest near Robbinsville is a great place to be awed by the splendor of virgin forest-a portion of the last one remaining in the eastern part of the nation. More than 60 miles of hiking trails are laid out to give visitors a taste of the varying terrain and ecology-from rock outcroppings and ridgelines to sheltered coves, quiet streams, and dramatic waterfalls. A true wilderness area for those who want to do back country hiking and camping.

**Joyce Kilmer Memorial Forest
Robbinsville / 828-479-6431**

Not to be outdone by the mountains, the state's coast is one of the most breathtaking in the nation. The Cape Hatteras National Seashore is comprised of the islands of Hatteras, Bodie (which is no longer a separate island, thanks to the naturally migrating topography of the Outer Banks), and Ocracoke. Called the "Graveyard of the Atlantic," this stretch of coast is the site of hundreds of historic shipwrecks. Shell hunting, sunbathing, swimming, fishing, kayaking, and canoeing are extremely popular. Back country camping is prohibited, but there are several developed campgrounds on the islands.

To avoid crowds, (or for those like Jessica who think they don't like the beach because of the sun, heat, and bugs), try visiting during the off season. The sunsets are just as beautiful, and the sound of the waves will still lull you to sleep in each other's arms.

Cape Hatteras National Seashore
Manteo / 252-473-2111

Merchants Millpond State Park in Gatesville gives you a southern cypress swamp at its best. (Our husbands both love swamps, and we admit that we've come around to the idea of swamps as eerily romantic.) At Merchants Millpond, you can take in the quiet beauty as you paddle your canoe under the tupelo gum trees with their elegant draping of Spanish Moss. If you go in the early spring, it actually may not be that quiet—a serenade of peepers awaits you.

Merchants Millpond State Park
Gatesville / 252-357-1191

In the central part of the state, Pilot Mountain State Park near Mount Airy offers dramatic cliff views, hiking and horse trails, and one of the most scenic stretches of the Yadkin River. You and your special friend can relive a little bit of childhood as you trade memories of your favorite *Andy Griffith Show* episodes: the fictional town of Mayberry was based on Griffith's hometown of Mount Airy, and Pilot Mountain inspired the name of the make-believe town of Mount Pilot.

Pilot Mountain State Park
Pinnacle / 910-325-2355

Hammocks Beach State Park, located almost entirely on coastal Bear Island, is the perfect place for a secluded sojourn with your loved one. The island is the coast in microcosm: maritime forest, salt marshes, and sand dunes, all within 890 acres. Accessible only by ferry (which, in combination with a winter water taxi service, operates year-round), the island is pristine and absolutely undeveloped. And it is never crowded—the ferry's passenger capacity ensures that only a limited number of visitors are on the island at any given time. So you will be free to enjoy swimming, fishing, shell hunting, birding, and camping in peace.

Hammocks Beach State Park
Swansboro / 910-326-4881

At Crowders Mountain, near Charlotte, view sheer cliffs over 150 feet tall, rent a canoe and paddle together on the lake, or try to catch a bass for dinner. The park is a bird watcher's paradise: more than 160 species have been spotted there, including a variety of waterfowl, songbirds, hawks, fowls, and woodpeckers. Rock climbers, who are advised to check in with the ranger station upon arrival, will find good climbing in a wide range of difficulty levels.

Crowders Mountain State Park
Kings Mountain / 704-853-5375

LAKES

If the sight of flat water and miles of shoreline and the prospect of a little water play are what you seek on a scenic day trip, we suggest a visit to one of North Carolina's recreational lakes. There are many in the state, and we have chosen to highlight just a few here. They offer a variety of recreational opportunities, including swimming (allowed on many but not all lakes), fishing, boating (including rentals), and picnicking. Many of these lakes are also natural bird habitats, so bring your binoculars.

Jordan Lake in Apex is home to two nesting pairs of bald eagles. We are told that in the summer months, more eagles can be seen on the lake than in any other area in the eastern part of the country. When you aren't tempted by eagle sightings, rent a canoe and seek out some of the more secluded coves. If the weather is warm, go in for a dip, then sun yourself dry.

**Jordan Lake State Recreation Area
280 State Park Road / Apex
919-362-0586**

With 40,000 surface acres of water, Lake Mattamuskeet is the largest natural lake in North Carolina, although it is only knee-deep in most places. Every fall and winter, it hosts huge numbers of migrating ducks, geese, and swans. Bald eagles, peregrine falcons, and osprey have also been spotted there.

**Mattamuskeet National
Wildlife Refuge
Swan Quarter / 252-926-4021**

You and your lover can find a little bit of everything (other than public swimming) at Lake Norman and its four associated parks, near Charlotte. The lake comprises more than 520 miles of shoreline and is the largest human-made lake in the state. Jetton Park features a sunning beach, picnic decks overlooking the water, formal gardens, and a gazebo. On the weekend, tandem bikes are available for rental. For fishing, try the pier at the smaller Ramsey Creek Park, and at Blythe Landing, you can play sand volleyball, have a picnic, or chase each other on rented personal watercraft. Paddleboat, canoe, and kayak fans will want to try Latta Plantation Nature Preserve. And if you prefer to let someone else do the work, take a cruise around the lake on the Catawba Queen, a classic paddlewheel riverboat. For a more personal touch, you can arrange a custom charter of a sailboat or yacht, with full crew, through Lake Norman Yacht Charters.

Jetton Park
19000 Jetton Road / Cornelius / 704-896-9808

Ramsey Creek Park
Nantz Road / Cornelius / 704-896-9808

Blythe Landing
NC Highway 73 / Cornelius / 704-896-9808

Latta Plantation Nature Preserve
Beaties Ford Road / Huntersville / 704-875-1391

Queens Landing
1459 River Highway / Mooresville / 704-663-2628

Lake Norman Yacht Charters
Cornelius / 704-542-5492 / www.lakenormancharters.com

In the foothills, Lake James State Park offers swimming and fishing, canoe rentals, and six miles of nature trails. Camping is also available at secluded walk-in sites, some right at the water's edge. You and your sweetheart can have the feeling of privacy that backwoods camping offers without the long walk!

🌲 **Lake James State Park**
NC Highway 126 / Nebo / 828-652-5047

Burlington's Lake Macintosh is a peaceful retreat where you can enjoy paddleboats and rowboats or fishing on more than a thousand acres of water. Swimming is not permitted and there are no hiking trails around the 61 miles of shoreline because of right-of-way issues. However, you and your date will appreciate the quiet—no motorized "personal watercraft" are allowed.

🏕 **Lake Macintosh**
Burlington / 336-538-0896

OTHER SCENIC DESTINATIONS

Owned and protected by the Nature Conservancy, the Nags Head Woods Preserve is a unique ecosystem that includes familiar Outer Banks sand dunes, a remnant of maritime forest, and freshwater wetlands. Take a walk along the Preserve's four miles of trails to look for abundant wildlife.

🗼 **Nags Head Woods Preserve**
301 West Ocean Acres Drive / Kill Devil Hills / 252-441-2525

Whiteside Mountain is a sight to behold: striped granite cliffs 750 feet tall—among the tallest cliffs on the east coast. An easily followed trail from the parking area deposits you at the top, where you will be rewarded with spectacular mountain views and maybe

a glimpse of a soaring peregrine falcon. It is a superb picnic spot—
and only a short drive from Cashiers and Highlands.

🌲 **Whiteside Mountain**
US Highway 64 between Cashiers and Highlands

COVERED BRIDGES

There's something charmingly old-fashioned about covered
bridges. They bring to mind a bygone era when the pace of life
and travel were slower. Just two covered bridges remain in North
Carolina, and both are well worth a visit. Apparently, any covered
bridge was known as a "kissing bridge," because lovers could steal
a kiss while riding through in their buggy. Plans are underway to
refurbish the Pisgah Covered Bridge, originally built in 1910, and
the turn-of-the-century Bunker Hill Covered Bridge has already
been restored.

Pisgah Covered Bridge
US Highway 220 over the Little River / near Asheboro
336-626-0364 or 800-626-2672
www.VisitRandolph.org

Bunker Hill Covered Bridge
US Highway 70 / (2 miles east of Claremont) / 828-465-0383

ROMANTIC LEGENDS

*Life has taught us that love does not consist in gazing at each other but in
looking outward together in the same direction.—Antoine de Saint-Exupery*

Any romantic likes a good love story, and there are several places in
North Carolina that have great love legends attached to them.
Fortunately, most of them are also lovely (if you can forgive the

pun) places to visit. To take in the mountain air (and a good story), consider the town of Blowing Rock, in Watauga County. There, you will find a dramatic cliff jutting out into the wind over Johns River Gorge 3,000 feet below. The view is spectacular, and the romantic legend adds a touch of historical drama. According to the story, a pair of young Indian lovers came to the blowing rock, where the man, torn by a conflict of duty and love, leaped into the abyss. His beloved prayed for his return, until one day, a great gust of wind blew him back onto the rock and into her arms. It is said that from that day onward, the wind has blown upward from the gorge below.

While you are in town, be sure to visit the charming downtown district, with its many quality craft and antique shops. In spring and summer, we suggest visiting the ice cream shop and strolling up the block to the public park, where you can sit on benches overlooking the main street and watch the world go by.

🌲 **Blowing Rock**
828-295-7111

Like Blowing Rock, Jump Off Rock provides panoramic mountain views and has a similar story. A Cherokee maiden who was distraught over the death of her chief leaped to her death off the rock. Legend has it that on moonlit nights you can see her ghost. (Thus far, these romantic legends are a bit morbid! But don't be deterred. These are beautiful vistas.)

🌲 **Jump Off Rock**
end of Laurel Park Highway, five miles from Hendersonville

Did you think Charles Frazier made up Cold Mountain? Well, the award-winning Civil War novel is fiction, but the mountain is real. In fact, there are three Cold Mountains in North Carolina, but the folks at the Canton Papertown Association assure us that the one in the Pisgah National Forest is the Cold Mountain of the book. The peak is not particularly accessible, as it is in a rugged wilderness area with only one blazed trail along its slopes. If you are interested in making this strenuous hike, check in with the Pisgah National Forest Ranger Station near Brevard. They can provide you with the maps you'll need. However, you can also gaze at the mountain from the overlook at Milepost 411.85 on the Blue Ridge Parkway.

🌲 **Cold Mountain**
Pisgah National Forest / Brevard / 828-877-3265

🌲 **Canton Papertown Association**
36 Park Street / Canton / 828-648-7925

Sunset Beach is home to the Kindred Spirits mailbox. Yes, a mailbox. Start walking hand-in-hand with your sweetie at the Sunset Beach pier. Walk a mile or so south and you will come to a bench on a sand dune overlooking the waves. Next to the bench is a mailbox, labeled Kindred Spirits, with paper and pencil provided. Take a moment to compose a note to leave for the kindred spirits who will follow you after you. Before you leave this enchanted and contemplative spot, take time together to read together the messages left by others before you.

🗼 **Kindred Spirits Mailbox**
Sunset Beach

Bridal Veil Falls in Macon County is romantic on several counts. First, like most waterfalls, its dramatic beauty gives it an air of romance. Second, true to its name, this particular one looks like a broad, delicate wedding veil of lace. But the name is also taken from a traditional Cherokee legend that any maiden who passed behind the waterfall would be married the following spring. You can even drive under this fall. On a hot day, with the windows and sunroof open, it might be more fun than catching the bouquet.

 Bridal Veil Falls
US Highway 64 / approximately 2.5 miles west of Highlands

WATERFALLS

Are waterfalls romantic? They must be, since Niagara Falls is a perennially popular honeymoon spot. But you don't have to go to the Canadian border and join hundreds of tourists at a designated observation deck to enjoy falling water together. Several especially attractive falls are listed below, but there are literally hundreds in the state. For a good guide to them all, see *North Carolina Waterfalls: Where to Find Them and How to Photograph Them* by Kevin Adams.

Dry Falls, near Highlands in Macon County, is so-named because, like Bridal Veil Falls, you can walk behind the sheer curtain of water (which falls from 80 feet) and remain completely dry.

Dry Falls
US Highway 64 / approximately 3.25 miles west of Highlands

The 404 feet of Hickory Nut Falls can best be viewed from Chimney Rock Park. Plunging into Hickory Nut Gorge, the falls were featured in the final fight scene in the romantic historical movie, *The Last of the Mohicans*. To add some romance to a visit to this spectacular waterfall, rent the movie first. It'll put you in the mood (to see the waterfall).

Hickory Nut Falls
Chimney Rock Park / Lake Lure / 828-625-9611 or
800-277-9611 / www.chimneyrockpark.com

Looking Glass Falls near Brevard will also be familiar to *Last of the Mohicans* fans. Deservedly, it is one of the most visited waterfalls in the state. Easily viewed either "up close and personal" or from the car, it's not to be missed.

Looking Glass Falls
US Highway 276 North / approximately 5.5 miles from Brevard

Schoolhouse Falls, in Panthertown Valley near Cashiers, is a special treat because of the unspoiled and uncrowded beauty of Panthertown itself. The walk to the falls is particularly enchanting during wildflower season.

Schoolhouse Falls/Panthertown Valley
Breedlove Road / Cashiers

At 411 feet, Whitewater Falls ranks as the tallest cascade east of the Rockies. Need we say more? Visiting it during the peak glory of fall color might inspire you to take up photography, painting, or poetry.

Whitewater Falls
NC Highway 281 / approximately 8.5 miles south of Cashiers

LIGHTHOUSES

The lighthouses along North Carolina's barrier islands (known as the Outer Banks) each have a distinctive look, but they share a common history of treacherous storms and countless ship wrecks in the waters they shine upon. Visiting one of these landmarks will give you and your lover, friend, or companion a window onto coastal life in days past and a taste of what the beach has always offered-beauty, the romance of the sea, and the feel of warm sand under your bare feet. We've chosen to mention only a few of these coastal jewels.

To really get a feel for the bygone days of lighthouses, visit Bald Head Island, where you won't find a single automobile. The island's most revered symbol and historic landmark is Old Baldy, an 1817 lighthouse commissioned by Thomas Jefferson. Visitors can climb to the top and enjoy the view below.

Old Baldy
Bald Head Island / 910-457-5003

At 150 feet tall with broad black and white horizontal stripes, the Bodie Island Lighthouse is not open for climbing. However, the keeper's quarters have been restored and serve as a visitors center that is open year-round. (By the way, it's pronounced "body.")

Bodie Island Lighthouse
Nags Head / 252-441-5711

Cape Hatteras Lighthouse, which measures 208 vertical feet, is the nation's tallest lighthouse and a treasured landmark that is on the National Register of Historic Places. Regrettably, it has recently been closed to the public as it is being moved to save the structure from the ever-encroaching waves. (We hope your love is solid as a rock—but don't count on the shifting sands of barrier islands.)

Cape Hatteras Lighthouse
Buxton / 252-995-4474

You are welcome to spend some time alone together atop the 158-foot Currituck Beach Lighthouse, in Corolla. Unlike its siblings along the Outer Banks, this lighthouse was left unpainted in natural red brick.

Currituck Beach Lighthouse
Corolla / 252-453-8152

The Cape Lookout Lighthouse sports an attractive black-and-white diamond paint job, but a look from the outside is all that is allowed the public. There are no roads on the three uninhabited barrier islands that make up the Cape Lookout National Seashore, which can be reached only by private boat or toll ferry. However, the beauty of the area will make the trip well worth the effort, and we're sure you'll both appreciate the privacy and quiet.

Cape Lookout Lighthouse
Harkers Island / 252-728-2250

GEM MINING

You may be surprised to learn that North Carolina was home to the nation's first gold rush, nearly fifty years ahead of California. For something silly to do together, try panning for gold or gems at the many mines that are open to the public. Think of it as a way to be children together, splashing in the creek, scooping up rocks and mud, and searching for buried treasure. But don't count on finding anything suitable for that engagement ring: although an

88-carat emerald was recently discovered in a working mine in Hiddenite, you should expect to find only tokens at the recreational mines listed below.

Reed Gold Mine was the site of the first documented discovery of gold in the United States. It is now a state historic site, and portions of the underground tunnels have been restored for guided tours. During the summer, you can also try your hand at panning for gold.

Reed Gold Mine State Historic Site
9621 Reed Mine Road / Stanfield / 704-721-4653

For a truly unusual outing, visit Castle McCulloch in Jamestown, near Greensboro. Imagine yourselves living in another era, members of royalty, as you stroll through the formal gardens of this former gold refinery built in the style of a medieval castle. Then see if you find gold and jewels as you pan at the on-site mine!

Castle McCulloch
6000 Kersey Valley Road / Jamestown / 336-887-5413
www.castlemcculloch.com

An on-site gemologist will help you evaluate your haul at the Nantahala Gorge Ruby Mine.

Nantahala Gorge Ruby Mine
14260 US Highway 19/74 West / Bryson City / 828-488-3854

The Old Pressley Sapphire Mine was the source several years ago of the record-setting, 1,445-carat "Star of the Carolinas" and the 1,035-carat "Southern Star." You never know what you might find in your sluice.

Old Pressley Sapphire Mine
240 Pressley Mines Road / Canton 828-648-6320

ALTERNATIVE FORMS OF TRANSPORTATION

Sometimes half the fun of a trip is getting there. So, instead of just taking a hike or going horseback riding (with picnic supplies stuffed into a backpack or saddlebags) how about going on a llama trek and letting the llamas carry along gourmet provisions? Wind Dancers Llama Treks is located on 270 acres of wilderness adjacent to Pisgah National Forest. Groups of four to six people (so you'll want to hook up with another couple or two, or ask the proprietors to match you up) will lead llamas to a wilderness picnic spot, complete with deck and waterfall. There, the wine, cheese, and chicken ready for grilling will be unpacked as you take in the scenery. Our sources say that there is even a bit of romantic background music—the llamas tend to "hum" as they walk along. (We don't know what you may have heard about llamas, but these are sweet, gentle, and full of personality.)

🌲 **WindDancers Llama Treks**
1966 Martins Creek Road / Clyde / 828-627-6986
www.winddancersnc.com

Taking to the air in a plane can be a dramatic way to make your love soar. On an airborne tour of the coast, the two of you can see the dunes, water, and sky as you've never seen them before. A range of plane types is available, including seaplanes and antique biplanes, and you can choose from a variety of different tours— even night flights!

🗼 **Kitty Hawk Air Services**
Wilmington International Airport / Wilmington
910-791-3034

(more next page)

🔦 **Kitty Hawk Aero Tours**
Kitty Hawk / 910-441-4460

🔦 **Aeronautics**
Wilmington International Airport / Wilmington
910-763-4691

ANNUAL SKY EVENTS

If you don't want to get off the ground yourself, or if your companion has a fear of flying, you can still enjoy some skyward adventures. The annual Rogallo Kite Festival at Nags Head is held in June. Bring your own kite and join in the fun, or just spectate. It's a great way to feel like a kid again. Or for a terrific off-season trip to the coast, take in the Kites with Lights show put on by Kitty Hawk Kites at the Jockey's Ridge dunes the first weekend in December. You'll be treated to the sight of lit stunt kites flying to the tunes of favorite holiday songs.

🔦 **Rogallo Kite Festival**
Nags Head / 800-334-4777 / www.kittyhawk.com

🔦 **Kites with Lights**
Nags Head / 800-334-4777 / www.kittyhawk.com

Burlington's annual Hospice League Balloon Fest is held the third week of May at the Burlington-Alamance Regional Airport. Watch hundreds of hot air balloons sail across the sky. You can go on a piloted ride, too, or arrange to have a declaration of love attached to one of the balloons.

🏛 **Hospice League Balloon Festival**
Burlington / 336-570-1444 or 800-637-3804

spotlight

THE BLUE RIDGE PARKWAY
The Most Romantic Road in America

Hugging the crest of the Blue Ridge Mountains, the Blue Ridge Parkway links Virginia's Shenandoah National Park with the Great Smoky Mountains National Park of western North Carolina and eastern Tennessee. Our friend poet Michael McFee calls the Parkway the most romantic road in America, and we heartily agree. The route is closed to all commercial traffic, which makes a tremendous difference as you and your sweetheart drive along serenely taking in the breathtaking scenery or stop for a quiet moment at one of the many scenic overlooks.

As Jessica and Scott have found over the years, it is easy to plan a long weekend together using the Parkway as your organizing principle. Your entire trip can be made without leaving the Parkway—even for gas, meals, and lodging (including camping). Or, you may drop into nearby towns to visit points of interest, then pick up the Parkway again to continue your excursion. As you drive, you will be spending some quality time in conversation with each other, unencumbered by distractions other than the spectacular views. Along the way, you will encounter countless picnic spots, scenic overlooks, waterfalls, and hiking trails, ranging from quick leg-stretchers to half-day (or longer) back-country hikes.

The many natural highlights along the Parkway are too numerous to mention, but we'll try anyway. Mount Mitchell (Milepost 355.4) is the highest point east of the Mississippi, with the kind of panoramic views you would expect from such a lofty height. Grandfather Mountain (in Linville, Milepost 305.1) is a privately owned nature preserve that features the famous Mile High Swinging Bridge. Walk with your darling across this suspension footbridge and don't let go of each other!

Another favorite wilderness spot is Craggy Pinnacle (Milepost 364.1), along a section of the Parkway known as Craggy Gardens. The Craggy Pinnacle Trail will lead you to a rhododendron forest atop a rocky peak. It can be a very private spot: you may feel like the only humans for miles around, which certainly has its appeal for lovers.

spotlight

THE BLUE RIDGE PARKWAY
The Most Romantic Road in America

Finally, a discussion of the romantic aspects of the Parkway must include Waterrock Knob (Milepost 451.2), the highest point to which you can hike on a Parkway trail. Far removed from the lights of mountain communities, this area is perfect for stargazing, even if you don't hike the steep half-mile trail to the top. Kiteflying is also popular in the grassy field at the parking lot.

For a change of pace from outdoor pursuits, visit the Folk Art Center (Milepost 382), just east of Asheville. Operated by the Southern Highland Craft Guild, the Folk Art Center is a gallery of first-rate crafts and functional art objects. Jessica and Scott make a special point to visit before special gift-giving occasions. The woodwork, glasswork, and pottery are especially irresistible.

Whether you go for spring wildflowers (which shouldn't be picked), summer berries (which can be), or fall foliage, the Parkway won't disappoint you. However, if you are planning a trip during the winter, be advised that bad weather often forces the closure of affected sections of the Parkway, and most of the campgrounds and lodging facilities are open only from May through early October.

🌲 **Blue Ridge Parkway**
828-298-0398 / www.blueridgeparkway.org

🌲 **Mount Mitchell State Park**
Burnsville / 828-675-4611

🌲 **Grandfather Mountain**
Linville / 828-733-4337 or 800-468-7325
www.grandfather.com

🌲 **Folk Art Center**
Asheville / 828-298-7928
www.mainsrv.main.nc.us/shcg/fac.html

Playing
Around

My love for you is more athletic than a verb.—Sylvia Plath

In the previous chapter, we hinted at the many possibilities the Tar Heel state offers for outdoor recreation: lakes for paddleboating, waterskiing, or just sunbathing, walks or jogs on white sandy beaches, mountain trails to explore. For those lovers who are drawn to more extreme sporting activities, we offer some options here.

If you're the kind of couple that likes to sweat together, you probably already have some favorite jogging or biking routes, so our aim here is to take you to some particularly scenic parts of the state—and, perhaps, to introduce you to some new sports activities.

We open with the state's bicycling highway system and with ways of getting to interesting biking destinations by train. For a truly romantic biking adventure, rent a tandem bike and ride it on the bicycle trails of the Outer Banks. If you prefer four legs to two wheels, we note several stables that rent horses or offer guided horseback tours. For winter sports fans, we list several skiing areas in the western part of the state.

We also suggest a number of boating adventures, from strenuous whitewater rafting trips to a calmer "waft" down the Eno River, including a unique weekend that combines daytime canoeing or kayaking with overnight stays in a comfortable bed and breakfast. Other water sports include snorkeling and scuba diving. We even offer you a way of taking to the air (hang gliding) before bringing you back to earth for the simple pleasure of a game of croquet.

Finally, a note for tennis and golf fanatics. Our "Let's Spend the Night Together" chapter, which highlights romantic lodgings, includes a listing of "Resorts for Sports" just for you.

BICYCLING

With its miles of country roads and pleasant climate, North Carolina is a great place to bike. To help you choose a bicycling route, the state Department of Transportation has designated a system of Bicycling Highways consisting of ten different routes that cover 3,000 miles of lightly traveled highways. If the two of you are serious bikers, you'll want to tackle the 700-mile Mountains to Sea route. If you start in the difficult mountain stretch, you can reward yourself at the end of your trip with a dip in the ocean. For couples who are more casual bikers, there are plenty of shorter routes to travel together. The DOT also has available maps to designated bike trails all over the state and a helpful brochure listing campgrounds found along the Bicycling Highways.

**North Carolina Bicycling Highways
DOT / Raleigh / 919-733-2804 /
www.dot.state.nc.us/transit/bicycle/**

If you'd like to travel across the state before starting your bicycling trip, Amtrak offers a "Bikes on Board" service on its Piedmont route. The Piedmont travels daily between Raleigh and Charlotte, with stops in Cary, Durham, Burlington, Greensboro, High Point, Salisbury, and Kannapolis. For a small handling fee, your bike will travel on a specially designed rack while you relax and let someone else do the driving. Advance reservations are required. On other trains that run through the state, you can check a boxed bicycle at staffed stations.

"Bikes on Board"
Amtrak / 800-USA-RAIL (872-7245)
www.bytrain.org/bike.htm or www.amtrak.com

Biking at the beach is a great way to spend some time together. The terrain is generally flat, the climate moderate, and the scenery spectacular. The Dare County Tourism Bureau produces a brochure that lists scenic bicycling routes including both roadways and some dedicated bike paths.

Dare County Tourism Bureau
Manteo / 252-473-2138 or 800-446-6262
www.outer-banks.com/visitor-info

If you don't want to bring your bike to the beach, there are a number of rental stores. Ocean Atlantic Rentals has four locations along the Outer Banks and will deliver your bike anywhere between Corolla and Hatteras. For a truly romantic ride, this is where you can get a tandem bike! (Beachgoers, take note: they also rent beach umbrellas, chairs, cabanas, grills, and coolers.)

Ocean Atlantic Rentals
Corolla, Duck, Nags Head, and Avon / 800-635-9559
www.outer-banks.nc.us/ocean-atlantic-rentals

You'll both have to be in tip-top shape to bike in the mountains, but if you are, you'll be rewarded by stunning scenery. And remember—for every uphill, there's a corresponding downhill. Based in Waynesville, Blue Ridge Cycling Adventures offers bike rentals and guided tours. You can book a private tour for just the two of you (plus the guide, of course). These tours range from half-day trips with one meal included to overnight trips of up to a week. You'll spend every night in a bed and breakfast, and you'll have earned the massage you each get during the trip. Popular destinations include the Blue Ridge Parkway, Hot Springs, and the rural mountain roads of Haywood County.

 Blue Ridge Cycling Adventures
Waynesville / 800-824-1168

HORSEBACK RIDING

If you dream of galloping along the beach or riding off into the sunset together, North Carolina offers plenty of opportunities for you. According to Martha Branson Holden in *Horseback Trail Riding Guide to North Carolina*, you can ride on established trails in most national and state parks and on parts of the Cape Hatteras National Seashore. It's best to call these parks in advance to find out about any restrictions; in particular, most of them don't have campgrounds that cater to horseback riders.

If you like the fantasy of riding the coast on horseback, Buxton Stables offers a guided beach ride-but be aware that this ride is only available to experienced English riders. If you're not experienced, opt for the one-hour trail ride through nearby woods; your horse will never go faster than a walk. You can also rent horses here, and take lessons during the off-season.

Buxton Stables
NC Highway 12 / Buxton
252-995-4659

In the mountains, the folks at Smokemont Riding Stables say they see all kinds of couples, from "just-mets" to honeymooners and beyond. Although they offer many types of excursions, they recommend the two-and-a-half hour waterfall trip as a nice outing for couples; it's an eight-mile round trip into the deep forest to see waterfalls that you can't view from roadside. Since their rides attract a lot of youngsters in the summer, they suggest signing up during fall color season or in mid-May when the rhododendrons and mountain laurel are blooming.

Smokemont Riding Stables
US Highway 441 / Cherokee
828-497-2373

You'll also find riding information in the nearby sidebar about Tanglewood Park as well as in the "Let's Spend the Night Together" chapter under the category "Resorts for Sports." For additional information about horse rentals and stables,

nature trails and an arboretum to explore. The rose garden, with more than 800 rosebushes, is particularly romantic. And if you're happier watching sports than participating, Tanglewood is home to the Vantage Golf Tournament on the Senior PGA Tour and the annual Tanglewood Steeplechase.

At this point you're probably thinking you could spend a week at Tanglewood Park and not see or do everything. You can—and true to its motto, Tanglewood offers a variety of overnight accommodations, from the elegant Manor House Bed and Breakfast Inn to rustic cottages by Lake Mallard or a campground right within the park's boundaries.

Tanglewood Park
Clemmons
336-778-6300
www.tanglewoodpark.com

North Carolina Horse News maintains an extensive database on its website at www.nchorsenews.com.

SKIING

You don't have to go to New England or the Rocky Mountains to enjoy a skiing date; you'll find a handful of ski areas in North Carolina's mountains. Generally open from November to March, they employ snowmaking equipment to keep you skiing all through the season. Depending on where you live, you can make a day trip of it, or these ski areas will help you find nearby lodging for an overnight trip.

At 5600 feet, Ski Beech Ski Resort bills itself as the highest ski resort in the eastern United States. The fourteen slopes are lighted for night skiing, and there is a dedicated slope for tubing; you can rent skis or snowboards or buy new ski togs together at one of the shops at Beechtree Village.

🌲 **Ski Beech Ski Resort**
1007 Beech Mountain Parkway / Beech Mountain
800-438-2093 / www.skibeech.com

Near Blowing Rock and Boone, Appalachian Ski Mountain boasts nine slopes and five lifts. Their French-Swiss Ski School offers private lessons as well as special beginners' packages. On Valentine's Day and New Years Eve, take a moonlight spin around the outdoor skating rink before a fireworks display. And note that if you're short on funds, there is free skiing on opening day.

🌲 **Appalachian Ski Mountain**
940 Ski Mountain Road / Blowing Rock / 800-322-2373
www.appskimtn.com

BOATING

We love because it is the only true adventure.—Nikki Giovanni

Canoeing, kayaking, and rafting are all great ways for couples to spend time together and to explore issues of trust and teamwork in a relationship. Whether you're experienced at these sports or want to learn, we have some great suggestions, from whitewater to still water. Almost anywhere there's a river or a lake, you'll find an outfitting company that will rent you the boat of your choice and give lessons or tours. We've chosen just a few of these companies that have the most interesting and comprehensive offerings.

The French Broad River is a mecca for whitewater fans. Depending on the time of year and on which stretch of river you choose, you can experience either roaring rapids or more serene currents that allow you to take in the scenery of the Pisgah National Forest. Blue Ridge Rafting offers four-mile, eight-mile, and overnight trips, with a professional guide in every raft. The Nantahala Outdoor Center has similar offerings on the French Broad and Nantahala Rivers as well as outings in "ducks"—inflatable one-person kayaks. Be sure to enjoy a meal at NOC's restaurant, Relia's Garden, after your adventure.

🌲 **Blue Ridge Rafting**
   Hot Springs / 800-303-RAFT (7238)
   www.blueridgerafting.com

🌲 **Nantahala Outdoor Center**
   Bryson City / 828-488-2175 or 800-232-7238
   www.nocweb.com

You don't have to worry about missing the beautiful scenery during your raft trip when you embark on the Great Smoky Mountain

Railway's Raft 'n' Rail trip. Departing from either Bryson City or Andrews, take a one-way trip to the Nantahala Gorge, then raft back down the Nantahala River to your starting point, where you'll find very welcome hot showers and changing facilities. A picnic lunch is included on this seven-hour excursion.

 Raft 'n' Rail
Great Smoky Mountain Railway
Dillsboro / 828-586-8811
or 800-872-4681 / www.gsmr.com

If you like the idea of a weekend canoe or kayak trip but don't like the idea of sleeping under the stars, Rock Rest Adventures has several overnight trips to the coast that combine a day of paddling with a night in a bed and breakfast. On one such trip, you'll travel by canoe through the swamps of the Roanoke River. Or you can take a sea kayaking trip to Masonboro Island or Ocracoke Island. In each case, your guide will point out interesting and endangered wildlife and plant species, and at the end of the day, you have a firm mattress, hot shower, and delicious meal awaiting you. (If you're real outdoor types, camping overnights are also available.) Rock Rest is based in Pittsboro and also offers lessons in canoeing and kayaking at nearby lakes.

 **Rock Rest Adventures**
Pittsboro / 919-542-5502

Here's a great option for romantics who may be too out of shape for whitewater or overnight paddles. Based at Durham's West Point on the Eno, naturalist "River Dave" Owen takes groups on moonlight wafting trips down the Eno River. Yes, that's wafting with a "W," and as the name implies, it's a kinder and gentler approach to river travel. River Dave says that almost no skill is needed to guide an inflatable kayak, and moreover, he points out that everyone is more beautiful in the moonlight. Call ahead for reservations, because these trips only take place for the three to five days around the full moon, and they are popular! (Daytime wafting trips are available, too.)

Eno River Wafting
West Point on the Eno / 5101 North Roxboro Road / Durham
919-471-3802

Moonlight tours—as well as sunrise and sunset tours—are also offered on the coast by Ocracoke's Ride the Wind Surf and Kayak. Explore this island's shoreline and the nearby Pamlico Sound by kayak with a guide who will instruct you in handling the kayak as well as pointing out the wildlife and environmental features of this saltwater habitat. Tours generally last three hours, and experienced kayakers can rent boats for longer trips.

Ride the Wind Surf and Kayak
NC Highway 12 / Ocracoke / 252-928-6311
www.ocracoke-nc.com/ridethewind

Another gentle approach to river travel is the "quietwater" river trip offered by Southern Waterways in Asheville. You won't see a bit of whitewater as you float past the Biltmore Estate, which means you'll be able to look for river otters, blue herons, and pileated woodpeckers that are common along this stretch of the French

Broad River. Sunset trips along this route are particularly lovely.
Note for mature romantics: ask about the senior citizen discount.

Southern Waterways
521 Amboy Road / Asheville / 828-232-1970 or 800-849-1970
www.paddlewithus.com

SCUBA DIVING AND SNORKELING

Learning to scuba dive or snorkel together can be a great experience. You don't have to be a super-athlete to learn to dive; in fact the only conditions that would exclude you are asthma or a fear of being underwater. The North Carolina coast offers watery adventures to both beginning and experienced divers. In addition to unique underwater ecosystems, the greatest offcoast attraction is the Graveyard of the Atlantic, an area off the Outer Banks with hundreds of sunken ships, many of them victims of World War II. Divers come from all over the country to explore these shipwrecks that are in our own backyard.

Serving the northern Outer Banks, Sea Scan Dive Centre offers classes in scuba diving from entry level to advanced, and also teaches snorkeling and skin diving (which involves holding your breath for a long time). According to the folks at Sea Scan, many couples take their classes together. Sea Scan also leads diving tours to all of the nearby shipwrecks; along with your dive you'll get a good history lesson about the Graveyard of the Atlantic.

Sea Scan Dive Centre
2600 South Virginia Dare Trail / Nags Head
252-480-FINS (3467) / www.netnc.com/seascan

Farther south in Morehead City, Olympus Diving Center has received positive notice in *Rodale's Scuba Diving* magazine. Night diving and deep river diving are among their training offerings, in addition to basic scuba and snorkeling classes. Shipwreck tours are also available, as well as equipment purchase and rentals.

Olympus Dive Center
713 Shepard Street / Morehead City
800-992-1258 / www.olympusdiving.com

Very experienced divers interested in visiting off-the-beaten-track wrecks will want to hook up with the BFDC, a dive club that organizes small group dives to shipwrecks that are not accessible for less experienced divers. These dives are not for beginners, but if both of you are advanced divers, you'll be rewarded with sights that few people have seen.

BFDC
Butner / 919-575-9033 / ias.ga.unc.edu/~egapmh/BFDC.HTML

Although we've focused on coastal outfitters here, dive shops and clubs offering classes are located throughout the state. A good source of information on these organizations can be found online at ncscuba.com.

HANG GLIDING

Not for the faint-of-heart or out-of-shape, hang gliding is an exhilarating experience, and where better to try this sport than at the birthplace of flight? With instructors from Kitty Hawk Kites, you'll learn to take a solo flight off the top of Jockey's Ridge, one of the largest sand dunes around. If hang gliding seems too solitary or extreme, the two of you can buy or rent a regular kite from these folks and take it to the beach for earthbound fun.

Kitty Hawk Kites
Nags Head / 800-334-4777 / www.kittyhawk.com

OUR KIND OF SPORT

Anyone can be passionate, but it takes real lovers to be silly.—Rose Franken

If you are not particularly athletic but are inspired by this chapter to participate in sports as a twosome, we've got a great suggestion for you. Go to your nearest locally owned sporting goods shop or mega-chain discount store and buy a croquet set. Review the rules, then find a nearby park (or your own backyard) and get playing. College lawns and quadrangles during spring and summer break provide terrific croquet terrain.

You need no athletic skills or coordination at all—in fact it's the unathletically goofy shots that provide a lot of the fun. It's particularly amusing to "send" your partner (you can think of all kinds of ways to apologize later). The exhibitionists among you can dress in regulation white and attract a crowd, but beware—they might want to horn in on your game!

Love
in the
Bleachers

Too much of a good thing is wonderful.—Mae West

What's a section that includes football and hockey doing in a guidebook to romantic North Carolina? This is a tricky category because watching a ball game is not as inherently romantic as attending the symphony. Or is it? Many people find ballet on the basketball court, art in a baseball diamond, and poetry in the sight of a galloping thoroughbred. A trip to the coliseum, the ballpark, or the racetrack can be a great date if—and this is very important—both members of the couple are equally avid fans. And if that's the case, once again North Carolina comes through for you, with such a variety of spectator sports that you can find a game to attend just about any day of the year.

We start with the well-known college athletic teams, pointing out that men's basketball is not the only game in town; women's basketball, men's and women's soccer, and many other college sports are easier to get tickets for and just as exciting. Minor league baseball has always been a favorite for dates, but now we also have professional women's softball and soccer. And the big leagues—NFL, NBA, WNBA, and NHL—have also come to North Carolina.

A more elegant spectator sport is the steeplechase, and we direct you to two annual horseracing events that support charities. Sometimes sporting events are fun for their celebrity-watching potential, and we suggest two charity golf tournaments with plenty of stargazing opportunities. Finally, for the couple that is truly committed to their favorite team and to each other, check out our sidebar on broadcasting your marriage proposal or declaration of love on your team's scoreboard.

COLLEGE SPORTS

We start with college sports because in North Carolina, they rule; professional major-league sports are still playing catch-up. Such is the intensity of fandom in college athletics that some readers will be surprised to find that this book's coauthors remain on speaking terms despite the fact that they fall on opposite sides of the great Duke/Carolina basketball divide. A romantic relationship with the same division of loyalties might be doomed, but if you both follow the same team you've overcome a major compatibility test!

North Carolina is home to four Atlantic Coast Conference schools, fielding championship teams in basketball, soccer, tennis, and much more. Men's ACC basketball is probably the most popular spectator sport in the state, but women's basketball and both men's and women's soccer at ACC schools are enjoying newfound attention in recent years. And you're more likely to get tickets to the latter! (Note to the romantically impaired: it is *not* romantic to sit home and catch the Heels or Deacons on television with a six-pack and a bag of chips.)

Duke University Blue Devils
Durham / 919-681-BLUE (2583) or 800-672-BLUE (2583)
www.goduke.com

University of North Carolina Tar Heels
Chapel Hill / 919-962-2296 / www.goheels.com

North Carolina State University Wolfpack
Raleigh / 919-515-2106 / www.gopack.com

Wake Forest University Demon Deacons
Wake Forest / 336-758-DEAC (3322) or 888-758-DEAC (3322)
www.wakeforestsports.com

Outside of the ACC, East Carolina University usually fields a powerful football team, Western Carolina University is competitive in baseball, and UNC-Charlotte excels in basketball.

East Carolina University Pirates
Greenville / 252-328-4500 or
800-DIAL ECU (342-5328)
www.ecupirates.com

Western Carolina University Catamounts
Cullowhee / 800-34GO WCU
(344-7938)
www.wcu.edu/athletics

UNC-Charlotte 49ers
Charlotte / 704-547-4949
www.uncc.edu/athletics

squad. (Hugo really seems more appropriate in this context.) The Piedmont Boll Weevils and other ball clubs will follow up a proposal with a "S/he said yes" message, always a fan favorite. The Winston-Salem Warthogs report that historic Ernie Shore Field has hosted two wedding ceremonies as well as countless proposals.

In order to broadcast your love, you just need to call the community relations or marketing office to arrange the details; please give them a week or two of notice. Some teams charge a fee, which usually goes to charity.

MINOR LEAGUE BASEBALL

Love is the only game that is not called on account of darkness.

—M. Hirschfield

Minor league baseball has always been a strong presence in North Carolina. From the Winston-Salem Warthogs to the Kinston Indians, you can always find a team playing nearby during the summer. You don't even have to be a huge sports fan to attend a baseball game. Part of the fun is just sitting outside with someone you love (or like), drinking beer, eating ballpark food, and talking. If your relationship is new, you can alternately watch the game and exchange childhood stories and favorite movies. If the date isn't going well, you can cover awkward silences by focusing on the game.

The best-known minor league team is the Durham Bulls, immortalized in the Kevin Costner/Susan Sarandon film *Bull Durham*. The Bulls recently moved from the beloved but shabby Durham Athletic Park to the new brick-and-green-paint Durham Bulls Athletic Park (or the D-Bap, as the local sportscasters call it), and they've been elevated to AAA status. But fans of *Bull Durham* will be relieved to hear that the snorting bull that appeared as a prop in the movie now presides over left field, sporting a "Hit Bull, Win Steak" sign, and it still lights up and snorts smoke after every Bulls home run.

Durham Bulls
Durham / 919-956-BULL (2855) / www.dbulls.com

Asheville Tourists
Asheville / 828-258-0428

Burlington Indians
Burlington / 336-222-0223

Carolina Mudcats
Zebulon / 919-269-2287
www.minorleaguebaseball.com/teams/carolina

Charlotte Knights
Fort Mill, SC / 704-357-8071 / www.aaaknights.com

Greensboro Bats
Greensboro / 336-333-BATS (2287)
www.minorleaguebaseball.com/teams/greensboro

Hickory Crawdads
Hickory / 800-488-3237 / www.unifour.com/crawdads

Kinston Indians
Kinston / 800-334-5467 / www.cl.org/baseball/kinston

Piedmont Boll Weevils
Kannapolis / 704-932-FANS (3267) / www.bollweevils.com

Winston-Salem Warthogs
Winston-Salem / 336-759-2233 / www.warthogs.com

WOMEN'S SOFTBALL AND SOCCER

If you long for the old Durham Athletic Park, you can catch the Durham Dragons there. The Dragons compete in the Women's Professional Softball League, as do the Carolina Diamonds, who play out of Sims Legion Park in Gastonia. Another women's pro team to follow is the Raleigh Wings, 1998 soccer champions in the W-1 League.

Durham Dragons
Durham / 919-680-FAST (3278) / www.durhamdragons.com

Carolina Diamonds
Gastonia / 704-865-3747 / www.carolinadiamonds.com

Raleigh Wings
Raleigh / 919-848-8412 / www.raleighwings.com

MAJOR LEAGUE PRO SPORTS

In recent years, the sports scene in North Carolina has become even more exciting with the addition of major league professional teams: The Charlotte Hornets (NBA) and the Carolina Panthers (NFL) have both flirted with postseason championships. In the Charlotte Sting, North Carolina scored one of only 10 WNBA teams; the Sting fell just short of playing in the 1998 championship game. The Carolina Hurricanes (NHL) are a relative newcomer; playing in Greensboro for their first two years, they move to a permanent home in Raleigh in 1999. Tickets to these games can be expensive, so be sure your date is equally devoted to the sport before spending the big bucks.

Charlotte Hornets
Charlotte / 704-424-9622 / www.nba.com/hornets

Carolina Panthers
Charlotte / 704-522-6500 (Charlotte TicketMaster)
www.cpanthers.com

Charlotte Sting
Charlotte / 704-357-0252 / www.wnba.com/sting

Carolina Hurricanes
Raleigh / 919-467-PUCK (7825) or 888-NHL-TIX1 (645-8491)
www.caneshockey.com

If you want to learn more about hockey with your favorite "little hockey puck," the Hurricanes offer Hurricane University. Over three days, you'll get on the ice with Hurricanes players to learn the basics of skating and hockey skills, get classroom instruction on the rules of the game, and attend a Hurricanes game at which you'll get to meet and talk to referees.

Hurricanes University
Raleigh / 919-467-7825

STEEPLECHASE

If you've ever longed to don semi-formal clothes and weird hats to go to Ascot Races, take heart: steeplechase racing has come to North Carolina. It involves thoroughbred horses, jockeys, speeds of up to 30 miles per hour, and hurdles up to five feet high. As many as five races take place on a given day, and there's plenty of time between races to socialize with your date or to place a private bet—just between the two of you—on the outcome of the next race.

The Charlotte Steeplechase, an annual benefit race held in the beautiful countryside outside of the Queen City, features five races on one April Day, culminating in the Bank of America's Queens Cup. Proceeds benefit Hospice of Union County and Carolina's ALS Center Endowment. If you want to get to know the horsey crowd better, make time for the Taste of the 'Chase Gala on the evening preceding the race.

Charlotte Steeplechase
Union County / 704-423-3400 / www.queenscup.com

The Brookhill Steeplechase is also a benefit event, sponsored annually in May by the Raleigh Jaycees. With purses of up to $50,000, this event attracts top jockeys and thoroughbreds. Between races, get away from the crowds by wandering Brookhill Farm's wooded property or taking a walk around the 20-acre lake.

Brookhill Steeplechase
Brookhill Farm / Clayton / 919-838-1492
www.brookhillsteeplechase.com

CELEBRITY GOLF TOURNAMENTS

For some people, attending a major sporting event is a thinly disguised excuse for celebrity watching. If you're both into stargazing, you'll be happy to know about two celebrity golf tournaments that take place annually in North Carolina. Keep in mind that like the steeplechases, these are charity events, so ticket prices may be higher than you expect. But you'll be rewarded by glimpses of, or even autographs from, top stars of sports and entertainment.

The Jimmy V Celebrity Golf Classic honors the late, charismatic North Carolina State University basketball coach Jim Valvano, who died of cancer in 1993. Entertainers like Kevin Costner, Susan Anton, and Sharon Lawrence join sports figures like David Robinson, Steve Rice, and Mia Hamm on the golf course to raise money for cancer research. More than 30,000 spectators descend on the golf course at Cary's Prestonwood Country Club, so don't expect to do your celebrity watching in private!

Jimmy V Celebrity Golf Classic
Cary / 919-319-0441 / www.golfclassic.org

You can't get much more celebrated than Michael Jordan! The former NBA star is honorary chairman of the Michael Jordan Celebrity Golf Classic, held each June in Greenville to benefit the Ronald McDonald Houses of North Carolina. Besides MJ himself, celebrity sightings in the past have included basketball star James Worthy, model Carol Alt, and actors William Devane, Kathie Lee Crosby, and Jamie Farr.

Michael Jordan Celebrity Golf Classic
Greenville / 252-353-4785
www.sportsline.com/u/jordan/offcourt/mjgolfclassic.html

See also the sidebar on Tanglewood Park in the "Playing Around" chapter for an additional steeplechase and pro golf tournament.

spotlight

GET A LITTLE WILD
AT THE NORTH CAROLINA ZOO

A trip to the Zoo—officially, the North Carolina Zoological Park—is a perfect excursion for couples in that "wanting to get to know you better" stage of the relationship. For a few months, you've been going out to dinner and a movie on weekends with perhaps a midweek date, and you may have been enjoying sleepovers. Now you want to see what it's like to spend an entire day with your sweetheart, and the Zoo fits the bill nicely. Centrally located in Asheboro, it's a great day trip from almost any part of the state.

The North Carolina Zoo was the nation's first "natural habitat" zoo: all the park's animal environments are as close to nature as possible. Five miles of pleasantly winding walkways link the habitat areas. These features make the Zoo a great place to stroll together on a pretty day. Share a bag of popcorn as you wander through Africa and North America (the two continents represented thus far in the zoo's exhibits). There's also a free tram if your feet get too sore from walking.

Lovebirds will find good company at the R. J. Reynolds Forest Aviary, housing tropical birds and plants in a display that is truly breathtaking. This is one exhibit in which you are actually in the habitat rather than looking at it, and you truly feel like you are on a birdwatching expedition in the rainforest. (The Aviary has been closed for renovations and will reopen in fall 2000.)

A recent addition to the Zoo is the Hummingbird Garden. Planted to attract and feed ruby-throated hummingbirds, this pretty garden features works of sculpture and a small courtyard with three stone benches—a perfect place to sit for awhile and watch the world go by.

The Zoo hosts several restaurants and a picnic area so that you can make a full day of it.

spotlight

GET A LITTLE WILD
AT THE NORTH CAROLINA ZOO

One of the functions of the Zoo's natural habitats is to encourage the animals to behave as in the wild. And they do! One day when Jessica and Scott visited, the zebra pair was enjoying a romantic moment. How your date reacts to such public displays of animal affection may be an interesting relationship barometer.

North Carolina Zoological Park
4401 Zoo Parkway / Asheboro / 800-488-0444 / www.nczoo.org

Take a
Walk
on the
Urban
Side

You have to walk carefully in the beginning of love; the running across fields into your lover's arms can only come later when you're sure they won't laugh if you trip.

—*Jonathan Carroll*

Strolling arm-in-arm with your date is a time-honored tradition that comes naturally to lovers of all ages. While previous chapters have suggested scenic spots for walks or hikes, here we highlight in-town strolls that don't require hiking boots: they are right where you live or where you are visiting, and they make for both enjoyable and inexpensive (or even free) dates.

Many cities have a downtown area devoted to galleries and artists' studios. Taking your companion on a gallery walk before or after a dinner on the town can set a relaxed and romantic mood for the evening. Wandering through downtown shopping districts and historic neighborhoods is also fun. But if you want to get away from the hubbub, we'll direct you to botanical gardens and even (gasp!) cemeteries that are suitable for a romantic stroll— and where you're less likely to encounter crowds.

Because of the collective nature of much of what follows, we are in some cases unable to provide addresses and telephone numbers. Armed with a good map and directions from a tourism bureau, you'll have no trouble finding these areas.

GALLERY WALKS

Curious about the art world? Visiting a gallery can be a lot of fun whether or not you're in the market to buy anything. And going as

Romantic Biltmore House

Asheville's Biltmore House, completed in 1895, comes about as close to a storybook castle as you can get in a country without royalty. The largest home in America, Biltmore's 250 rooms are a breathtaking vision of luxury and beauty. The Estate's 8,000 acres (that's not a typo) feature gardens designed by Frederick Law Olmsted (whose other masterwork was Central Park). The glass and steel conservatory has recently reopened after an extensive renovation and now houses exotic plant species from around the world.

We suggest you devote at least a day to your visit to the Biltmore Estate. You will want to tour the house and gardens, which include not only the conservatory but also a romantic walled garden, a rose garden, and a bass pond. The Estate's winery is described in the next chapter, and the complimentary tastings there add an elegant touch to your visit.

Biltmore Village, the town that was built to house the army of workers who constructed and

a couple gives you the chance to get a sense of each other's taste. Seeing a studio is also a treat—a little like visiting backstage at the theater. Taking a walk through a gallery district can give you a taste of the community's arts scene. The organized gallery walks discussed below, many of which extend after regular business hours, give a bit more structure to your rambles. Think of these self-guided tours as open houses in which you are invited into the world of working artists.

The mountains of western North Carolina have attracted artists and craftspeople for generations. This legacy is apparent in the region's vibrant gallery scene. In Asheville, a downtown arts revival began in early 1990s, and the area now boasts more than 20 galleries. Several times each year, both Asheville and nearby Black Mountain celebrate their fine arts and crafts tradition by hosting gallery walks and studio open houses. Details and the sites included vary each year, so call for information.

 City Center Arts' Gallery Walk
Pack Square (and surroundings)
Asheville / 828-258-0710

 Artist's Studio Tour
Black Mountain / 800-669-2301

In historic north Charlotte, the Davidson Gallery Crawl has become a tradition every first and third Friday night of the month. Tour the Davidson Street neighborhood of working artists and visit the galleries that display their work, which ranges from prints to glassware, sculpture, photography, jewelry, and furniture.

Davidson Gallery Crawl
Davidson Street / Charlotte

Raleigh's Moore Square Arts District, occupying a three-block radius around historic City Market, includes nonprofit as well as commercial galleries. Artspace in downtown Raleigh is a visual arts center that comprises not only several galleries but also a collective working studio (which is open to the public) for forty artists. It serves as the hub of the monthly First Friday Gallery Walk, which includes galleries in Moore Square and, recently, in South Glenwood. Live music outdoors is part of the festivities in the summer.

Artspace
201 East Davie Street / Raleigh
919-821-2787
www.citysearch.com/rdu/artspace

First Friday Gallery Walk
Moore Square Arts District
Raleigh / 919-828-4555
www.raleighcvb.org/galleries.html

worked on the Estate, is a wonderful neighborhood for exploring on foot. Many distinctive shops and galleries await you. Of particular note is New Morning Gallery, which displays a marvelous array of fine crafts. High end, but with many affordable pieces, it is an ideal spot to find an inspired gift for your special someone. If your energy begins to flag during your stroll, stop for proper English tea, served daily at 3:30 at Chelseas and the Village Tea Room, before you continue your tour.

Biltmore Estate
Asheville
828-274-6333 or
800-624-1575
www.biltmore.com

New Morning Gallery
7 Boston Way / Asheville
828-274-2830

Chelseas and the
Village Tea Room
6 Boston Way / Asheville
828-274-0701

Gallery Row in Nags Head is a unique gallery district (sans organized tour) that celebrates the romance of the old United States Lighthouse Service. Inside a replica of the Point Fermin Lighthouse, you'll step back to the 1920s and find a treasure trove of lighthouse memorabilia. As you continue down the Row, which ends at the beach, you'll pass shops and galleries specializing in fine art, crafts, and jewelry. Once on the sands, stop to enjoy a moment alone together.

Gallery Row
Milepost 10.5 on Driftwood Street / Nags Head / 252-441-4232
www.seabeacons.com

In Winston-Salem, artists and craftspeople have renovated the old brick buildings of the historic downtown tobacco market and turned the area into a thriving neighborhood of studios and galleries, located next to the Visitors Center in the renovated City Market. Periodic downtown "Gallery Hops," which are held in the evenings near the intersection of Sixth and Trade Streets, feature more than twenty galleries and shops, including Artifacts, a new gallery specializing in African Shona sculpture. Refreshments are provided at stops along the tour.

Sixth and Trade Art District
Winston-Salem

Many of the artists of Waynesville open their studios to the public for a day in June each year, providing a unique opportunity to see works in progress and meet the artists. The tour includes galleries as well as studios. If you miss this annual event, you can still enjoy strolling through Waynesville's beautiful downtown and visiting the galleries there, many devoted to fine mountain crafts.

Downtown Studio and Gallery Tour
Haywood County Arts Council / 114 Church Street
Waynesville / 828-452-0593

SHOPPING AND DOWNTOWN STROLLING

At the risk of making a sexist distinction, we have to ask if any man can be convinced that shopping might be romantic? Well, yes, it can be, especially the kind of relaxed window shopping we suggest. Rest assured that we are not talking about malls and outlet centers. In addition to unique shopping centers, North Carolina's historic downtowns are great places to spend a day browsing or buying with your sweetheart.

In historic Wilmington, begin your walk along the cobblestone streets of Chandler's Wharf, a collection of shops and restaurants at Water and Ann Streets. Walking a few blocks east along the Cape Fear riverfront, you'll arrive at the Riverwalk, a boardwalk that follows the river. You can look out at the *Battleship North Carolina* across the river, and you'll pass the *Henrietta II* (which is featured in our "Feeding Your Love" chapter); during the summer, some restaurants across Water Street have live music. Then make your way to the Cotton Exchange, another shopping and dining area, and the first district in downtown Wilmington to adapt historic buildings to new uses. Nearby, you'll also find a neighborhood of old, stately homes and gardens. Some of the homes have public tours, which you may wish to pursue. Otherwise, just take in the ambiance.

Historic Downtown Wilmington
Wilmington / 910-341-4030 or 800-222-4757

Chandler's Wharf
Ann and Water Streets / Wilmington / 910-815-3510

Cotton Exchange
North Front and Grace Streets / Wilmington / 910-343-9896

As you walk through historic New Bern, you can step back in time 300 years. As mentioned in the "Arts for the Heart" chapter, Tryon Palace served as the capitol of the Colony of North Carolina, and a tour of the grounds is highly recommended. The self-guided Heritage Tour will take you past more than 100 historic structures on Governor's Walk, a unique shopping and dining district that comprises the historic downtown area.

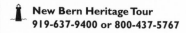
New Bern Heritage Tour
919-637-9400 or 800-437-5767

Governor's Walk
New Bern / 919-637-9400 or
800-437-5767

Scarborough Faire is the unusual and engaging shopping district of Duck, at the north end of the Outer Banks. You'll find food, toys, crafts, books, art, and more as you stroll on winding boardwalks under the trees. More than 20 shops and restaurants give the area its unique and extremely friendly character—a potent antidote to the megamall shopping experience. Scarborough Faire is a gathering place for visitors and residents alike.

Scarborough Faire
Duck Road (NC Highway 12) and
Christopher Street / Duck

---

highlight

Replacements, Ltd.

When things have gotten serious and you and your loved one are ready to take vows—or just set up housekeeping together—you will most likely go through the ritual of choosing china and silver patterns. For the supershoppers among our readers, we have a suggestion. Go to Replacements, Ltd., in Greensboro. The size of four football fields (guided tours are available every half-hour), this famous store has every conceivable pattern, including those that have been discontinued. But more fun than that is the museum of more than 2,000 unique pieces of china, porcelain sculpture, glassware, crystal, and silver. Think of it as combining a shopping trip with a visit to a first-rate museum.

Replacements, Ltd.
1089 Knox Road
Greensboro
800-REPLACE (737-5223)

Historic Edenton, settled in the early 1700s on the Albemarle Sound, has the reputation of being the prettiest town in the state. As you stroll, you'll want to browse through the many boutiques and antique shops. Guided walking tours are available through the visitors center, if you want to add a bit of structure to your visit. Or if your feet need a rest, hitch a ride on the trolley that circumnavigates downtown.

Historic Edenton
800-775-0111

Historic Downtown Hendersonville, near Asheville, heralds itself as exemplifying the best of Smalltown USA. Home to many antique stores, a vintage toy shop, an old-time pharmacy, and a restored 1905 Mast General Store, Hendersonville is a great downtown for walking. You can also steal a kiss from your friend as you sit on one of the many downtown benches and watch a small piece of the world go by.

Historic Downtown Hendersonville
Main Street / 800-828-4244

Greensboro's State Street Station is located in what was once part of McAdoo Heights, a small mill village at the turn of the century. Start a leisurely visit with cappuccino and scones, then move on to shopping for flowers (always romantic), jewelry (can't go wrong there), fine stationary (invitations, perhaps, to an upcoming ceremony?) or designer clothing. End your day with a meal, a bottle of wine, and live music at one of the many restaurants nearby.

State Street Station
between Church and Elm Streets / Greensboro / 336-230-0623

Old Salem is an example of a living history museum at its best. Costumed interpreters recreate life in what was an 18th-century community of Moravians in North Carolina. An admission ticket is required for entry into the many demonstration buildings and gardens, but it is well worth the cost. You will also want to explore the Museum of Early Southern Decorative Arts, have dinner at the Old Salem Tavern, and take home a treat to share from the wood-fired oven at Winkler Bakery.

Old Salem / Museum of Early Southern Decorative Arts near the intersection of Interstate 40 (business) and US Highway 52 / Winston-Salem / 336-721-7300 or 888-OLDSALEM (653-7253) / www.oldsalem.org

GARDENS

North Carolina's stunning and varied natural beauty is mirrored in the state's many botanical gardens. These gardens offer a perfect opportunity to surround yourself with beauty as you enjoy an afternoon together. If you both have an interest in gardening, wonderful. But a green thumb is completely unnecessary to your enjoyment of these horticultural delights. Bring a picnic and settle in together. (If there is a special ceremony in your future, think about a garden as a venue: inquire about regulations and availability.)

As you'll see, our listings are not all-inclusive: we have chosen to focus only on a selection of gardens that represent particularly romantic environments. If you are curious about a garden not included here, by all means, test its romantic potential on your own!

Fayetteville's Cape Fear Botanical Garden is a beautiful destination any time of year. Its 85 acres include formal gardens, forest land, a natural amphitheater, and a grand gazebo on the Great Lawn. (If you are watching your pennies, the $2 entry fee is waived on the first Saturday of each month.)

Cape Fear Botanical Garden
536 North Eastern Boulevard / Fayetteville / 910-486-0221

Coker Arboretum is an oasis in the middle of the University of North Carolina campus in Chapel Hill. In just five acres, there are nearly 600 species of trees and shrubs, planted along winding paths that offer remarkable privacy in such a busy university community. In fact, there is so much privacy that you might want to make a little noise as you approach secluded spots, so as not to "disturb" any other couple. Jessica and Scott enjoyed many a lunch-time picnic here when they both worked in Chapel Hill. It's amazing how romantic a cheese sandwich can be under the right circumstances!

Coker Arboretum
North Carolina Botanical Garden
Raleigh Street / Chapel Hill / 919-962-0522

If you want a garden experience that's a little bit out of the ordinary, we suggest you visit the "Maize Maze" near Winston-Salem. Elsewhere we've mentioned the incredible variety of outdoor pursuits available at Tanglewood Park in Clemmons, but a four-acre maze made of growing corn is clearly the most unusual. Escape together, or pursue each other, as the mood strikes you. (The maze is open only during corn season, July through September.)

Amazing Maize Maze of Tanglewood
Clemmons / 336-778-6300 / www.tanglewoodpark.org

The Elizabethan Gardens on Roanoke Island, near Manteo, offer a more traditional botanical palette, but with the added color of history. Called "a living memorial to our first English colony," the

Elizabethan Gardens have a historic setting, a Gate House filled with period furniture and portraits, a variety of formal gardens as well as wildflowers, historical statuary, and a sixteenth-century gazebo. Beautiful year-round, the Elizabethan Gardens would make a great off-season coastal excursion.

Elizabethan Gardens
NC Highway 64 at Fort Raleigh
National Historic Site / Manteo
252-473-3234 / www.outerbanks-nc/com/elizabethangardens

The campus of the University of North Carolina at Charlotte boasts several romantic gardens. The Van Landingham Glen is a wooded natural garden featuring meandering paths amid a forest of rhododendron. Its location in a ravine makes it both cooler and more private than the surrounding campus. Adjacent to the Glen is the Susie Harwood Garden, which includes a Japanese garden and ornamentals from around the world. There is also a Sculpture Garden and a nearby lighted sculpture that makes for a perfect nighttime stroll.

Gardens at University of North Carolina at Charlotte
704-547-2000

The 17-acre Greensboro Arboretum located in Lindley Park features 2,500 species of trees, shrubs, and flowers beautifully displayed amid outsized sculpture. Don't miss the butterfly garden—formed in the shape of two butterflies joined by a fountain—which features flowers and plants that attract those who fly on gossamer wings. The beautiful exhibits are also a good source of practical ideas for the couple that wants to set up gardenkeeping together. The quietest corners are the gazebo in the winter garden and the wildflower trail. Benches and secluded picnic spots abound.

Greensboro Arboretum
Lindley Park / Wendover Avenue
and West Market Street
Greensboro / 336-373-2199

One of the state's best-known botanical gardens, Duke University's Sarah P. Duke Gardens, includes five miles of pathways and more then 2,000 plant varieties, including exhibit areas devoted to native plants and Asiatic species. An idyllic retreat, the garden is a perfect place to meander, have a picnic, toss a Frisbee, or read poetry to each other. In the spring, the early morning mist on the wisteria arbor is particularly enchanting. If you want to avoid the species *Undergraduatae suntannus*, visit the gardens during Duke's spring break or in the summer.

Sarah P. Duke Gardens
Anderson Street near Campus
Drive / Durham / 919-684-3698

Incredibly, another Dentzel carousel resides just 60 miles away, in Raleigh's Pullen Park. This 1911 model is also fully functional and open for rides. While at the park, you can also rent a paddleboat and tour the lake together, or enjoy a leisurely walk around it on the boardwalk while feeding the ducks.

For both parks, call ahead to confirm that the carousel will be operating when you want to visit.

Burlington City Park
South Church Street
336-222-5030

Pullen Park
520 Ashe Avenue / Raleigh
919-831-6468

Part of the Sandhills Community College campus and designed as a training field for horticulture students, the Sandhills Horticultural Gardens are a treat for nature lovers. Of particular romantic interest are the rose garden; the Atkins Hillside Garden, which includes five bridges, waterfalls, pools, and a gazebo; and the Desmond Native Wetland Trail Garden, which is a bird sanctuary traversed by a wooden boardwalk.

Sandhills Horticultural Gardens
2200 Airport Road / Pinehurst / 910-695-3882

To see the best of southern Appalachian horticulture, visit the North Carolina Arboretum in Asheville. The Arboretum's 426 acres include both formal and natural gardens, much undisturbed woodland, and several miles of walking and mountain biking trails. The gardens include the stunning Appalachian Quilt Garden, planted in the pattern of a traditional quilt. All outdoor areas remain open until 9 p.m. to accommodate lovers of sunsets and moonlight.

North Carolina Arboretum
100 Frederick Law Olmsted Way / Asheville / 828-665-2492

Each year, in early April, the North Carolina Azalea Festival in Wilmington heralds the arrival of spring by celebrating the azalea's stunning blaze of color. The four-day festival combines a street fair, local and national headline entertainment, art shows, garden tours, plant sales, and more. Whether your love is in full bloom, or just beginning to bud, you can't go wrong with this festival. You'll be in a crowd, but you are sure to have a good time, and you'll be together (which is the point, right?).

North Carolina Azalea Festival
Wilmington / 910-763-0905 / azalea.wilmington.org

CEMETERIES

Our friend Catherine Bishir, an authority on the state's historic architecture, first suggested to us the romantic possibilities of cemeteries. Located in pastoral settings, some cemeteries are—like gardens—oases of outdoor beauty and calm in the midst of urban areas. In addition, they generally afford visitors near-complete privacy. Historic graveyards are the most appealing: old headstones and monuments are often beautifully crafted, and some have wonderfully romantic inscriptions. We include here a few of these final resting places that we think offer something pleasant to living lovers.

Literature lovers may want to make a pilgrimage to historic Riverside Cemetery, which dates to the 1880s. Asheville's native son, Thomas Wolfe, best known for his novels *Look Homeward, Angel* and *You Can't Go Home Again*, is buried there, as is O. Henry. As you walk amid the unusually lovely monuments and markers in the cemetery, you can admire the huge, regal oaks that shade your path.

Riverside Cemetery
58 Birch Street / Asheville / 828-259-5800

For more on the Thomas Wolfe theme, buffs will enjoy a visit to Oakdale Cemetery in nearby Hendersonville. The beautiful angel monument of Italian marble that Wolfe refers to in *Look Homeward, Angel* is to be found here.

Oakdale Cemetery
US 64 West / Hendersonville / 828-693-9708

Another cemetery named Oakdale is located in Wilmington. A carefully landscaped graveyard dating to the antebellum era, it is a stunning sight to see in full bloom during spring and summer. It contains graves of many Confederate veterans, freemasons (in their own section of the graveyard), and members of Wilmington's historic Jewish community. There's even the grave of a woman buried—seated in a chair—in a giant barrel of rum. (She died at sea in 1857, and her body needed to be preserved.)

Oakdale Cemetery
520 North 15th Street / Wilmington / 910-762-5682

Calvary Episcopal Church and Churchyard is a superb example of antebellum Gothic Revival architecture situated in what looks like a botanical garden. One of the church's rectors in the mid-nineteenth century was an avid gardener with a particular passion for exotic species, and the churchyard bears the fruits of his labors. In *A Guide to the Historic Architecture of Eastern North Carolina* Catherine Bishir recounts a story of one visitor who chided the rector for making the churchyard so lovely that he was "enticing folks to die."

Calvary Episcopal Church and Churchyard
411 East Church Street / Tarboro / 252-823-8192

Beaufort's Old Burying Ground has been called one of the most beautiful spots in the city, in large part because of its setting amid majestic live oaks. It is one of the state's oldest maintained cemeteries, established in 1724, and its points of architectural interest include fine stone monuments and obelisks, brickwork markers, and iron fences. History buffs will be interested in the many historical figures laid to rest here, including Otway Burns, a privateer and hero of the War of 1812. The Old Town Restoration Complex provides guided tours; self-guided tours are also permitted.

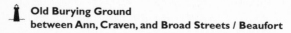

Old Burying Ground
between Ann, Craven, and Broad Streets / Beaufort

Feeding
Your
Love

The most important things to do in the world are to get something to eat, something to drink and somebody to love you.—Brandan Francis Behan

A good part of any romance is conducted over a meal. Almost every first date involves dinner out, and finding out whether your new romantic interest shares your taste in food and drink is just as important as discovering whether you have the same sense of humor or taste in movies. Both of us chose the caterer for our weddings before we picked out wedding dresses, and almost everyone celebrates special anniversaries with a special meal.

We open this chapter by sharing a handful of especially romantic dining spots—including a few surprising "moveable feasts." These restaurants, known for exquisite menus and lovely ambiance, are perfect for impressing on a first date or celebrating special occasions. Then, for those who want to dine under the blue sky, we highlight a few purveyors of picnic foods, some of whom provide everything from the basket to the bug spray.

Beer and spirits are fine, but wine is the perfect libation for lovers. By visiting one of North Carolina's wineries, you can have a great excursion with your lover and bring home a delicious souvenir of your trip. If you don't know the difference between a sauvignon blanc and a cabernet franc, we steer you to a few wine outlets that offer winetasting courses.

Finally, for the couple that cooks together, we suggest spending a leisurely day gathering ingredients at area farmers markets and pick-your-own fruit farms and then cooking up a romantic dinner at home. Can't cook? We've got help. Finally, we suggest a couple of annual food-related festivals for a fun (but not very private) feeding frenzy.

DINNER OUT

We've spent a good part of this book trying to convince you that there are more creative dates than going out to dinner. But sometimes dinner at a nice restaurant is just the dating fix a couple needs. We had a dilemma: there are far too many great restaurants in North Carolina for us to list them all. So we've chosen just a handful of special dining spots to suggest; these are notable for their menus, beautiful settings, or romantic atmosphere. Be prepared—most of these great eateries fall in the "splurge" category!

Located on the causeway between Nags Head and Manteo, Basnight's Lone Cedar Café serves local seafood and game. Every window seat has a view of Roanoke Sound; our friend Annette Windhorn says to be sure to ask for one with a view of the sunset.

Basnight's Lone Cedar Cafe
7623 South Virginia Dare Trail / Nags Head / 252-441-5405
www.ego.net/us/nc/ob/lonecedar/

At the Beaufort House Restaurant, feast on seafood or steaks in an intimate space with candles, white tablecloths, and a waterfront setting. One Valentine's Day years ago, Lisa and Bill scored a window table overlooking the water and were treated to the sight of a black-crowned night heron posing on a nearby pylon.

Beaufort House Restaurant
502 Front Street / Beaufort / 252-728-3899

Elizabeth's Café and Winery is known for its pairings of wine and food; in fact *Wine Merchant* and *Wine Spectator* magazines have praised its wine list. Live jazz is offered some evenings.

Elizabeth's Café and Winery
Scarborough Faire / Duck / 252-261-6145

The only North Carolina restaurant to receive five diamonds from AAA, Fearrington House is simply superb. Enjoy a three-course fixed-price meal in one of several cozy dining rooms. A friend wrote us that her nephew arranged with the staff to delay dessert while he took his girlfriend for a stroll on the grounds and presented her with an engagement ring. Champagne was awaiting their return. Fearrington House is also a top-rated bed and breakfast.

Fearrington House
2000 Fearrington Village Center / Pittsboro / 919-542-2121

Located in Chapel Hill's Siena Hotel, Il Palio belies the myth that you should avoid hotel restaurants. As you are led through the vast, elegant dining room, each staff member you encounter will stop to welcome you. Such warm treatment lasts throughout your meal at this superb Tuscan restaurant. The price tag can be high, but the wait staff will help you decide how to combine the delicious appetizer, pasta, and main courses to your taste and budget. The next best thing to a trip to Florence!

Il Palio, Siena Hotel
1505 East Franklin Street / Chapel Hill / 919-918-2545
www.sienahotel.com

Some terrific chefs in Durham restaurants are making news with seasonal menus featuring fresh local ingredients, but Nana's wins our nod here because the dining room is also intimate and quiet. It's easy to pretend it's just you, your date, and the wait staff. If you want to be a bit more sociable, check out the monthly wine dinners, during which you can chat with winemakers and sample perfect pairings of food and wine.

Nana's
2514 University Drive / Durham / 919-493-8545

For a really intimate setting, request the private dining room at Greensboro's Paisley Pineapple. Located in the city's historic district (the building originally was home to a brothel!) this restaurant serves an eclectic menu that features game as well as classical dishes with southern overtones, including vegetarian fare. The sofa bar is the perfect spot for a flirtatious before-dinner cocktail or after-dinner port or coffee.

Paisley Pineapple
345 South Elm Street / Greensboro / 336-279-8488

Serving California cuisine and ethnic food, the Pewter Rose Bistro was recently rated by readers of *Creative Loafing* as the best Charlotte restaurant for a romantic meal. Their Sunday brunch is highly rated and a good way to experience this popular eatery without breaking the bank.

Pewter Rose Bistro
1820 South Boulevard / Charlotte / 704-332-8149

You don't have to play golf to experience the beautiful surroundings of the Springdale Country Club. Seated at the outdoor terrace at the SourWood Grille, you can enjoy a fabulous meal while taking in the surrounding mountain scenery. The menu is eclectic with an emphasis on wood-fired grilled items.

SourWood Grille at Springdale Country Club
200 Golfwatch Road / Canton / 828-235-9105 or 800-553-3027

MEALS ON WHEELS—OR WATER

We have discovered a couple of ways to share a meal while traveling over some of the most scenic parts of North Carolina. Leave your car behind and enjoy one of these "moveable feasts." Advance reservations and payment are required.

From April to December, you can take a dinner cruise up the Cape Fear River on the *Henrietta II,* an old-fashioned sternwheel riverboat. From downtown Wilmington, you'll travel up the Cape Fear River for two-and-a-half hours while enjoying a martini or bottle of wine and a festive dinner. After dinner—or between courses—you can dance to contemporary music or take in the riverside sights from the upper deck.

Henrietta II / Cape Fear Riverboats
Water Street / Wilmington / 800-676-0162

Similarly, the *Crystal Queen* sails out of Beaufort on a dinner cruise seasonally. Your cruise on this paddle wheeler will take you along the Intracoastal Waterway past the Morehead City waterfront, the Coast Guard Station, and Fort Macon, then out to Beaufort Inlet. During your three-course meal, a tour guide will provide commentary on these and other points of interest including, if you're lucky, dolphins diving in the distance. Your first course will almost certainly involve fresh seafood, but vegetarians take note: because of the logistics of catering on board, special meal requests cannot be taken.

Crystal Queen
600 Front Street / Beaufort / 252-728-2527

At the other end of the state, Lake Lure Tours offers a different take on the dinner cruise. Bring a bottle of wine and an appetizer on board for a cocktail-hour tour of this stunning mountain lake. After the sun sets, you'll be dropped off at one of several lakefront restaurants for a leisurely meal. Your return trip, under the light of the moon, is a good opportunity to snuggle with your sweetheart, particularly in the brisk autumn months. Lake Lure Tours provides the blankets.

Lake Lure Tours
Lake Lure / 828-625-0077 / www.lakelure.com

What could be more romantic than riding the rails through the rolling mountains? Nothing—unless you add a candlelight dinner with your favorite date. The Great Smoky Mountain Railway operates the Twilight Dinner Train from April to December. Over two-and-a-half hours, you'll be served a three-course meal from a seasonal menu; wine and cocktails are available. Enjoy the elegant ambiance of the reconditioned dining car, gracious service, fine china and crystal, and candlelit tables adorned with crisp linen tablecloths. In the fall, there are special wine and dinner excursions featuring the wine of a particular region paired with a four-course dinner.

Twilight Dinner Train
Great Smoky Mountain Railway
Dillsboro / 800-872-4681 / www.gsmr.com

Feeling committed to your relationship? If you're looking for a site for a "moving" wedding or commitment ceremony, each of these tour operators offers private charters.

Picnic Purveyors

North Carolina's moderate climate makes dining *al fresco* a great choice for much of the year. In previous chapters, we've suggested some favorite picnic spots, from secluded natural settings to outdoor venues where you can see a musical performance or film. You can put together your own picnic meal, but if you're cooking-impaired or short of time, one of these experts can do the work for you.

When we saw chocolate body paint listed on the Valentine's Day takeout menu at the Glass Onion Gourmet Market, we knew owner/chef Ed Kaminsky would have some good suggestions for a romantic picnic menu. He didn't let us down. He started with chocolate—"a known aphrodisiac," according to Ed. He pairs chocolate-covered strawberries with champagne or chocolate truffles with a dessert zinfandel. The folks at The Glass Onion will pack your chocolate and spirits along with salads and sandwiches of your choosing in a picnic basket complete with utensils, linens, and a corkscrew. If you don't know your date very well, Ed suggests that you request their special lovers' garlic- and onion-free salads. But here we disagree—if your date can't handle garlic and onions, why pursue the relationship?

The Glass Onion Gourmet Market
NC Highway 55 at High House Road / Apex / 919-362-1967

Laurey's Catering in Asheville will also pack a picnic basket for you, and they sent us several suggested menus. Since the Blue Ridge Mountains are close by, we particularly liked their suggestion for a hiking picnic that can be carried in your backpacks: trail mix to nibble during the hike, then a grazing meal of extra-sharp Vermont cheddar cheese, smoked trout paté, crusty French bread, ripe strawberries, and, of course, chocolate truffles. You can also have your meal packed in a traditional picnic basket, which you can buy or return.

🌲 **Laurey's Catering/Gourmet-to-Go**
67 Biltmore Avenue / Asheville / 828-252-1500
www.laureysyum.com

Cabbages & Kings is operated by the chef at the White Doe Inn in Manteo, but you don't need to be a guest at the Inn to order a picnic meal. A typical picnic might include sandwiches on focaccia, a fruit dish, and a savory cucumber and tomato salad incorporating herbs from the Inn's garden, along with bottled water, beer, or wine. Because of the warm temperatures, you can ask for your meal in an insulated container, or you can choose a basket or box. Whatever the packaging, when you open your container you'll find it adorned with flowers from the Inn—an aromatic touch that we like.

🗼 **Cabbages & Kings**
310 Sir Walter Raleigh Street / Manteo / 252-475-1110

At Mount Airy's Picnics to Go, you can choose between a lunch basket for two and a dessert basket for two. Being the way we are, we're intrigued by the dessert basket, which includes four desserts, a beverage, fruit, and candy. Utensils and linens are included, and the basket is yours to keep.

🏃 **Picnics to Go, c/o Merritt House Bed & Breakfast**
618 North Main Street / Mount Airy / 336-786-5810

SPECIALTY FOODS

North Carolina is blessed with hundreds of specialty and gourmet food shops, including some of the ones we just listed as picnic basket purveyors. Every large city and most small towns boast at least one gourmet or wine shop featuring prepared foods and cooking ingredients from every cuisine imaginable. We've chosen three very special shops to highlight here.

You can find cheese at just about any specialty market or super-market, but there is only one place in North Carolina where you can watch cheese being made. Using time-tested methods, the Ashe County Cheese Company makes mountain cheddar with fresh milk delivered from nearby dairies. For a fun outing with your date, you can stop by and watch the cheese-making process, then select from a choice of sharp, medium, or mild to bring home or add to your picnic basket. The retail shop also offers food items like jams, relishes, and smoked sausages.

Ashe County Cheese Company
Main and Fourth / West Jefferson / 336-246-2501 or
800-445-1378

Why buy your sweetheart Belgian chocolates when you can buy North Carolina chocolates? Using European methods and the finest chocolate available, Geldof Chocolatier makes scrumptious truffles and chocolates at their Raleigh chocolate factory. We espe-cially like the Carolina Critter box—four hedgehog-shaped chocolates with caramel and pecans. (Dark chocolate, please!) If you can't make it to Raleigh, you can order chocolates from Geldof's website.

Geldof Chocolatier
3512 Wade Avenue / Raleigh / 919-834-9188 / www.geldof.com

The granddaddy of North Carolina gourmet shops is A Southern Season. Established in 1975, this Chapel Hill institution has enormous selections of prepared foods, wines, coffees and teas, and cookware. You can also think of A Southern Season as Valentine's Day Central. They offer heart-shaped candies, cookies, gift boxes and baskets, wreaths-even a heart-shaped cheddar cheese coated appropriately in red wax. You and your sweetheart could spend a day exploring this food lover's paradise, but fortunately, they also ship. Online ordering is available.

A Southern Season
Eastgate Shopping Center / Chapel Hill / 919-929-7133 or
800-253-3663 (for orders) / www.southernseason.com

A JUG OF WINE . . .

It warms the blood, adds luster to the eyes,
And wine and love have ever been allies.—Ovid

If you fantasize about a romantic vacation for two in wine country, but can't pull together the time or money to travel there, have we got news for you! You don't have to go to Napa Valley to tour a vineyard and see wine being made. North Carolina has twelve wineries, stretching from the mountains to the coast, and most of them are open for tours and tastings. In fact, before Prohibition, North Carolina was the number one wine producer in the country. In those days, most North Carolina wine was made with the native scuppernong grape, but now many wineries are also offering dry, European-style wines. All of the wineries we list welcome visitors, but call ahead for their hours.

The most frequently visited winery in North Carolina-and probably the best-known wine producer-is the Biltmore Estate Winery.

If you tour Biltmore Estate, the Winery is worth a visit, but be aware that you'll have to pay an entrance fee. The winetastings are free, though.

🌲 **Biltmore Estate Winery**
Asheville / 828-255-1776

The well-known wine writer Robert M. Parker, Jr., wrote, "One of the South's best kept wine secrets is Westbend Vineyards. . . . As fine as these wines are, I am surprised they are not better known outside of North Carolina." Westbend produces a full line of European-style wines, including Chardonnay, Merlot, and Cabernet Sauvignon. Westbend's 45-acre vineyard is a stunning setting for the winery, tasting room, and gift shop. Take your wine purchase to the outside picnic area and enjoy!

🌲 **Westbend Vineyards**
5394 Williams Road / Lewisville / 910-945-5032
www.agr.state.nc.us/markets/commodit/horticul/grape/
westbend.htm

A visit to the Martin Vineyards on Knotts Island is a true adventure. After a 45-minute ferry ride, you can spend a day touring the vineyards and strolling the fruit orchards. (You can also arrange to pick your own grapes, apples, or peaches.) The tasting room overlooks Currituck Sound. Martin Vineyards offers scuppernong, European, and apple and peach wines.

🎣 **Martin Vineyards**
Martin Farm Lane / Knotts Island / 252-429-3542

For sheer scenic beauty, the Silohouse Vineyard and Winery is a good choice. When you see the grapevines planted on the rolling Blue Ridge Mountains (look for the silo in the middle of the vineyard), you could almost imagine you're in Europe. This small operation offers Chardonnay and Cabernet Sauvignon, and you should definitely call to make sure they are open before visiting.

🌲 **Silohouse Vineyard and Winery**
Walker Road / Waynesville / 828-456-5408

While space doesn't permit full descriptions, these wineries also welcome visitors. One of them may be near you!

🏠 **Bennett Vineyards**
6832 Bonnerton Road / Edward / 252-322-7154 or 800-801-9725

🏘 **Dennis Vineyards**
24043 Endy Road / Albemarle / 704-982-6090

🏠 **Duplin Wine Cellars**
Highway 117 / Rose Hill / 910-289-3888

🏘 **Germanton Art Gallery & Winery**
Route 1 / Box 1-G / Germanton / 910-969-2075

🌲 **North Carolina Waldensian**
1530 19th Street Southwest / Hickory / 828-327-3867

🌲 **The Teensy Winery**
3661 Painters Gap Road / Union Mills / 704-287-7763

🌲 **Villar Vintners of Valdese**
4940 Villar Lane Northeast / Valdese / 828-879-3202

For more information about North Carolina wineries, including maps and directions, visit the North Carolina Grape Council's website at www.agr.state.nc.us/markets/commodit/horticul/grape/.

WINETASTING CLASSES

Do you want to learn more about wine? Most gourmet shops offer free winetastings as a way to introduce customers to their line of wines. We're in favor of free samples, but because they're usually held on high-traffic weekends, most of these winetastings are not good forums for learning about wine—or for romance!

But there are some good opportunities to expand your knowledge of wine. There is a modest fee for each of these classes, and it's a good idea to find out whether food will be available or if you should eat first.

The Wineseller in Wilmington offers educational winetastings every few months, each with a theme: the wine of a particular country, wines from the same grape, and so on. Because they don't advertise these classes in the newspaper, stop by the store and ask to be added to the newsletter mailing list.

The Wineseller
801 South College Road / Wilmington / 910-799-5700

In Raleigh, the Seaboard Wine Warehouse also offers winetasting classes. Representatives of several distributing companies will explain the ins and outs of, for instance, Italian wines, while you sample the wines and nibble hors d'oeuvres.

Seaboard Wine Warehouse
800 Semart Drive / Raleigh / 919-831-0850

highlight

Home Alone

On a wintry night, what could be more romantic than dinner for two in front of your own fireplace? We have enjoyed this meal many times since Lisa and Bill learned how to make fondue from the owner of a Zurich restaurant. It's easy to make and a natural for couples: one person can grate the cheese and cube the bread while the other fixes the salad and prepares the fondue. And there's an old rule that anyone who drops their bread into the fondue has to kiss the person to their right.

For the price of dinner at an upscale restaurant, you can buy a nice fondue set to use over and over again.

CHEESE FONDUE FOR TWO

2/3 cup dry white wine
1/2 pound Gruyere cheese, grated
1/2 pound Appenzeller or Emmenthaler (Swiss) cheese, grated
3 tablespoons Kirsch (cherry liqueur)
1 teaspoon cornstarch
2-3 garlic cloves, minced
2 tablespoons onion or shallot, minced
1 loaf peasant or French bread, cut or torn into bite-sized pieces

>

Similarly, the Asheville Wine Market offers many introductory winetasting opportunities as well as classes on varietals such as red burgundy. They sometimes join with nearby restaurants for special wine dinners.

 Asheville Wine Market
65 Biltmore Avenue / Asheville
828-253-0060 or 800-825-7175

Finally, we have enjoyed wine classes offered by Duke University's Continuing Education program. Usually limited to fewer than fifteen people, these courses are popular among couples. As the evening wears on, you really get to know your classmates! Recent offerings have included "Wine 101"—an introduction to the basics of winetasting—and "The Wines of Alsace."

Continuing Education
Duke University / Bishop's House
Durham / 919-684-6259
www.learnmore.duke.edu/ShortCrs/

THE COUPLE THAT COOKS TOGETHER . . .

If you both enjoy cooking, spend a weekend day gathering ingredients for a romantic meal. Although you could shop at one of the gourmet markets we've already featured, a more carefree approach would be to visit one of North Carolina's many farmers markets or "pick-your-own" farms to choose fresh, seasonal ingredients. Can't cook? We've got help, in the form of two establishments that offer cooking classes. Finally, be sure to check out the sidebar "Home Alone" for a menu that you can cook together.

There are so many community farmers markets in North Carolina that we were unable to single out just a few. Instead, we're listing the year-round state-operated farmers markets. Check the food section of your local newspaper (usually on Wednesday) for additional local markets. At the state markets, you will find not only seasonal fruits and vegetables, but also flowers, jams and jellies made from local fruits, and baked goods. Most of these have restaurants on site, so get up at sunrise with the farmers, have breakfast, and shop early for the best produce.

Place the wine in a fondue pot and bring it to a boil on the stove. Stirring constantly, add the cheese a little at a time until it is melted. Mix the cornstarch into the Kirsch and add to the pot, along with the minced garlic and onion. Turn the heat to medium and continue to stir until the melted mixture has thickened some, about 5 minutes. Set the hot fondue on a table burner. Dip the bread cubes in and enjoy. The fondue should continue to bubble and thicken as you eat it. Serve with chilled white wine from the bottle you opened to prepare the fondue, a simple green salad, and perhaps some Geldof chocolates for dessert. The Swiss often add side dishes of prosciutto (we've substituted smoked salmon) and cornichons or other small, crisp pickles.

Charlotte Regional Farmers Market
1801 Yorkmont Road / Charlotte
704-357-1269

NC State Farmers Market
1201 Agriculture Street / Raleigh
919-733-7417

Piedmont Triad Farmers Market
2914 Sandy Ridge Road / Colfax
336-605-9157

Western NC Farmers Market
570 Brevard Road / Asheville
828-253-1691

If you want your produce even fresher than you can get at the farmers market, pick your own! From the coast to the mountains, you'll find hundreds of pick-your-own farms for strawberries, blueberries, tomatoes, corn, grapes, figs, and salad greens. Apples and peaches are grown all over the state, but Hendersonville is an apple-growing center, and you'll find especially rich pickings there. Most of these farms will also sell produce that they've harvested, and some offer other foodstuffs like cider and preserves.

Rather than list just a few of the many pick-your-own farms, we suggest you search the website maintained by the North Carolina Department of Agriculture and Consumer Services at www.agr.state.nc.us/markets/commodit/horticul/.

A different take on "pick your own" is available at the private clam beds of the Hatteras Village Aqua Farm. Harvest your dinner with rakes and buckets provided by this company—they guarantee your clamming success. If you don't want to get your feet wet, you can also buy fresh seafood from their shop.

Hatteras Village Aqua Farm
56406 NC Highway 12 / Hatteras / 252-986-2249

Finally, if you want to spice up your home cooking with flavorful herbs, consider an expedition to the Gourmet Garden Herb Farm in Weaverville. You can buy your own herb plants from the greenhouse or purchase herb mixtures and vinegars from the shop. Take a leisurely stroll through their extensive plantings of herbs and edible flowers to get ideas for your own herb garden.

Gourmet Gardens Herb Farm
14 Bankstown Road / Weaverville / 828-658-0766

If one or both of you is cooking-challenged, take heart. Cooking classes are offered in almost every city. Because cooking schools tend to come and go, we've listed just two very established ones here. But check the weekly food section of your newspaper to find a class that's right for the two of you. Some classes are hands-on and some are demos, so be sure to ask for details before you sign up. A fun birthday or anniversary gift would be a gift certificate for both of you to attend a cooking class.

Featuring both hands-on and demonstration classes, Roosters Gourmet Market and Gifts has a schedule packed with delicious learning opportunities. Local chefs and cookbook authors are often guest instructors, and the recent topics have included "Pastry 101" "A Simple Dinner Menu," "Italian Night," and "Understanding Chocolate."

Roosters Gourmet Market and Gifts
401 State Street / Greensboro / 336-272-2665

In Durham, Lan's Gourmet Foods, Gifts, and Chinese Cooking School offers beginner, intermediate, and advanced courses in Chinese cuisine by Lan Tan, who has taught Chinese cookery in New York and on cable television shows. Classes are participatory, and you'll enjoy a delicious meal afterwards.

Lan's Gourmet Foods, Gifts, and Chinese Cooking School
4201 University Drive / Durham / 919-493-1341

FOOD FESTIVALS

Almost every day in North Carolina, you can attend some sort of outdoor festival featuring crafts, food, music, and the obligatory 5K Fun Run. These can be enjoyable events, but we don't find the crowds, noise, and sweat terribly romantic. There are a few exceptions, though, including these two festivals for food lovers. If you attend one of these festivals, it won't be a quiet date, but it will be a scrumptious one.

Because of the oyster's romantic reputation, we can't resist telling you about the North Carolina Oyster Festival. Held every October in the coastal town of Shallotte, this festival has all the usual trappings of crafts and fun runs. Keep your focus on the food: shrimp, fish, and of course, oysters, served steamed by the bucket.

North Carolina Oyster Festival
Shallotte / 800-426-6644
www.southernfestivals.com/nc/oysters.html

In North Carolina, they say, barbecue is a noun, not a verb. And it's pork, not beef. Lexington calls itself the barbecue capital of the world, and it serves as host of the annual barbecue festival, also in October, that's been called "one of the top ten food festivals in the U.S.A." by *Travel & Leisure* magazine. Pig out!

Barbecue Festival
Lexington / 800-222-5579 / www.barbecuefestival.com

spotlight

FALL IN LOVE
AT THE STATE FAIR

When the State Fair comes to Raleigh, it might as well be October, to paraphrase the Oscar-winning song from the 1945 Rodgers and Hammerstein movie *State Fair.* Romance was in the air in that movie, and it can be for you, too, at the State Fair.

The Fair takes place over ten sultry fall days, and you could make several dates out of it. (We know one person who goes every single day!) With food, games, thrill rides, and entertainment, the Fair has something for lovers in every age group and income bracket.

Start out your evening at the midway, where you can win a stuffed animal for your date by showing off your skills at shooting hoops or tossing coins onto far-off plates. For the young or young at heart, you can give your honey some love taps in the Bumper Boat ride.

As you exit the midway, you'll encounter a real relationship-tester: people who will guess your age, weight, or birth month. You win another prize if they're wrong.

If you're brave enough to have your weight guessed in front of your date, be sure to do it before you head for the food booths, where you'll find classic State Fair fare: hot dogs, funnel cakes, roasted corn, cotton candy, Italian sausages with peppers and onions, elephant ears, apple dumplings, and, of course, North Carolina barbecue. Hint: do *not* share a ride on the roller coaster until you've digested your meal.

A great place to let your meal settle is in the livestock judging area. Particularly if you're city folks, you'll be entertained and enlightened as pigs, cows, and horses are shown and judged; we still get a kick out of one particular sow who was referred to as "well uddered." And if you can stand to think about food again, be sure to stroll through the area where pies and jellies are judged.

A free concert is offered every night of the Fair in Dorton Arena, and it's worth the price of admission alone. The emphasis is on country acts, with the likes of Garth Brooks, Laurie Morgan, Clint Black, and Alan Jackson, but R&B groups like the Temptations, Little Richard, and the Platters have also entertained at past State Fairs.

spotlight

FALL IN LOVE AT THE STATE FAIR

True, the Fair is crowded. But you and your loved one can steal a private moment— and a moonlit kiss—at the top of the double Ferris Wheel. And at the end of the evening, you can stand holding your date in your arms and watch the nightly fireworks show before you head home to make some fireworks of your own.

For folks in the western part of the state, the North Carolina Mountain State Fair has many of the same features as the Fair in Raleigh. It is held every September for ten days in Fletcher, near Asheville.

North Carolina State Fair
North Carolina State Fairgrounds / 1025 Blue Ridge Boulevard
Raleigh / 919-733-2145 / www.ncstatefair.org

North Carolina Mountain State Fair
Western North Carolina Agricultural Center
1301 Fanning Bridge Road / Fletcher / 828-687-1414
www.agr.state.nc.us/markets/fairs/mtnfair

A Night
on the
Town

You will find as you look back upon your life that the moments when you have really lived are the moments when you have done things in the spirit of love.
—Henry Drummond

Get dressed up, honey, we're going out! Whether you're in the mood for something festive or trying to get out of a two-person couch-potato rut, we suggest a night on the town. What follows is a sampling of some fun ways to spend the evening (in public) together. You can get a taste of casino life, enjoy a comedy act (we like to think the couple that laughs together stays together), take to the dance floor, or spend a literary or musical evening at a nearby bookstore.

For an extra touch of class, a limousine service can take you in style wherever you want to go. If you like, start your evening with dinner at one of the restaurants mentioned in or "Feeding Your Love" chapter.

LUCKY IN LOVE

"Love is the wild card of existence."—Rita Mae Brown

Feeling lucky? You don't have to go to Vegas or Atlantic City to try your luck in a casino. Harrah's Cherokee Casino has more than 2,000 video gaming machines on which you can play blackjack, poker, and craps. Your evening at Harrah's can include dinner in one of three restaurants (The Range Steakhouse is the best for

dates) and a performance at the 1,500-seat Cherokee Pavilion theater. True to the spirit of Las Vegas, Harrah's recently featured a
performance by Tom Jones. (Wayne Newton must surely be next!)
Other recent acts include Tanya Tucker and Bill Cosby.

🌲 **Harrah's Cherokee Casino**
    Cherokee / 800-HARRAHS (427-7247)

COMEDY CLUBS

Find out whether your date shares your sense of humor at a comedy club. These clubs feature nationally known acts that you'd
find on HBO or the Comedy Channel, including Brett Butler,
Sinbad, and Richard Jeni. Once, Robin Williams, who was filming
Patch Adams in nearby Chapel Hill, made an unannounced 45-
minute appearance at Charlie Goodnight's. Be sure to call ahead
for reservations.

🏘 **Charlie Goodnight's Comedy Club**
    861 West Morgan Street / Raleigh / 919-828-LAFF (5233)
    www.charliegoodnights.com

🏮 **Comedy Club, Ramada Inn**
    Milepost 9½ / Kill Devil Hills / 252-441-7232

🏘 **Comedy Zone**
    5317 East Independence Boulevard / Charlotte / 704-568-4242

🏘 **Comedy Zone**
    944 Bragg Boulevard / Fayetteville / 910-483-1272

🏘 **Comedy Zone**
    1126 South Holden Road / Greensboro / 336-333-1034

DO YOU WANT TO DANCE?

Judging by the number of studios offering classes, social or partner dancing has made a big comeback in recent years. We're talking about any kind of dancing in which the couple actually
touches, from ballroom dances such as the waltz and foxtrot to
Latin dancing and country western's two-step. Note for the rela-
tionship-impaired: singles can take classes from most of these studios. You might just meet your soulmate on the dance floor.

In cities throughout the state, Fred Astaire Dance Studios offers
private or group classes in swing, Latin, and ballroom dance, and
most of their studios also have social dances that are open to the
public. In Wilmington, for example, Fred Astaire has recently
opened the Lumina Ballroom, with a 3,000 square-foot dance
floor. Every weekend, live orchestras or disk jockeys play music
for the dancing public.

Fred Astaire Dance Studios
4714 Maple Avenue / Wilmington / 910-791-7229

2520 North Sharon Amity Road / Charlotte / 704-536-6070

4702 Garrett Road / Durham / 919-489-4313

5002-K High Point Road / Greensboro / 336-299-4977

20700 North Main Street / #120 / Cornelius / 704-892-0252

600 Town Centre Boulevard / Pineville / 704-889-8277

6166-A Falls of the Neuse Road / Raleigh / 919-872-0111

703 B-C Jonestown Road / Winston-Salem / 336-760-9930

The Blue Ridge Ballroom in Asheville and Carolina Dancesport in Durham also offer private and group lessons in the major social dances including foxtrot, waltz, rumba, cha cha, shag, and merengue, and both offer public dance parties several times a month.

Blue Ridge Ballroom
Newbridge Shopping Center / 55 Weaverville Highway
Asheville / 828-253-9108

Carolina Dancesport
2409 Guess Road / Durham / 919-416-9213
www.citysearch.com/rdu/dancesport

In Fayetteville, Roland's Dance Studio has the full gamut of classes, but for true romance on the dance floor, take their classes in Argentine tango, which they describe as a "two-and-a-half minute love affair."

Roland's Dance Studio
308 Hope Mills Road / Fayetteville / 910-424-0409

The tango and the two-step are great, but the official dance of North Carolina is the shag, a high-energy swing dance performed to beach music (just think of Motown acts like the Embers and the Drifters). Reds Beach Music in Raleigh is completely devoted to this dance craze; you can shag seven nights a week. They often feature live bands such as the popular Band of Oz, and they open an outdoor dance deck when weather permits. And they have "Single Mingle" nights.

Reds Beach Music
4400 Craftsman Drive / Raleigh / 919-876-733

Shag enthusiasts have formed clubs in almost every city in North Carolina, and if you want to find one near you, check out the website www.shagdance.com.

A LITERARY NIGHT OUT

All great lovers are articulate, and verbal seduction is the surest road to actual seduction.—Marya Mannes

Say you're not the dancing type of couple; you share quieter interests like books and poetry. Most bookstores now maintain a full schedule of author readings and musical performances. You'll be surprised at the number of nationally known authors who appear in North Carolina bookstores—and many of these authors call North Carolina home! Some bookstores now have cafes, so you can have dinner and entertainment or enlightenment (or all three) under one roof. Because of our common background in book publishing, we are particularly biased in favor of such literary dates.

Since poetry is the language of love, we particularly recommend First Tuesday Poetry Night at the Regulator Bookshop in Durham. Every month at least one area poet is featured. The Regulator also hosts non-poetry readings and talks several nights a week, and they have recently added the Java Café.

Regulator Bookshop
720 Ninth Street / Durham / 919-286-2700 /
www.regbook.com

Two bookstores in the western part of the state also have cafés and musical performances. In Sylva, City Lights Bookstore and Café hosts local musicians and author readings and presentations. Appalachian regional authors are a particular specialty. And the Café (a great dinner spot) makes the best portobello mushroom sandwich we've ever tasted. Malaprop's Bookstore and Café in Asheville also has a full schedule of author readings and musical performances that reflect the surrounding creative and alternative community.

> 🌲 **City Lights Bookstore and Café**
> **3 East Jackson Street / Sylva / 828-586-9499 or 888-853-6298**
> **www.citylightsnc.com**

> 🌲 **Malaprop's Bookstore and Café**
> **61 Haywood Street / Asheville**
> **828-254-6734 or 800-441-9829**

At the other end of the state, look for Manteo Bookseller's off-season reading schedule. From May through September, there is an author signing books in the store every Wednesday at lunchtime. But once the summer crowds disperse, there are weekend evening events in which authors read from or give presentations related to their books.

> 🗼 **Manteo Booksellers**
> **105 Sir Walter Raleigh Street / Manteo / 252-473-1221**

In the center of the state, Quail Ridge Books features weeknight readings and presentations by regional and nationally known authors. Quail Ridge really knows how to throw a book party: when Charles Frazier appeared to sign *Cold Mountain,* more than 1,000 copies were sold. Probably standing in a long line with your date is not your idea of romantic, but many events at Quail Ridge are on a more intimate scale.

> 🌳 **Quail Ridge Books**
> **3522 Wade Avenue / Raleigh / 919-828-7912**

In Durham, The Know specializes in books appealing to African Americans, and their reading calendar reflects that focus. Friday night jazz and Motown sets are also a feature at this store.

The Know
2520 Fayetteville Street / Durham / 919-682-7223

These bookstores also host readings:

Bristol Books
1900 Eastwood Drive / Wilmington / 910-256-4490

Dee Gee's Gifts and Books
508 Evans Street / Morehead City / 252-726-3314

McIntyre's Fine Books and Bookends
2000 Fearrington Village / Pittsboro / 919-542-3030

Page After Page Bookstore
Southgate Mall / Elizabeth City / 919-335-7243

Bookstores like **Borders**, **Barnes & Noble**, and **Books-a-Million** have wonderful coffee shops very active author reading programs, and some also schedule musical performances. They are located across the state. Be sure to check literary offerings from nearby colleges and universities as well. The best place to find out about literary events is in the free weekly arts tabloids published in most communities or on the Sunday book page of larger newspapers.

GETTING THERE IN STYLE

So you've planned your special night on the town. Whether you're dancing, hitting a comedy club, or attending a literary event, get there safely and in style by letting someone else do the driving. There are, of course, many more limousine services than we could mention here.

In Greensboro, Fantasy Limousines will pick you up in a 1920 convertible roadster, one of their two Rolls Royces, or a forty-foot stretch limo complete with a bedroom!

Fantasy Limousines
Greensboro / 336-674-0591 / www.fantasylimo-nc.com

People will take notice when you travel through the Research Triangle area in the 1935 Rolls Royce Phantom II from Highland Classic Limousine and Shuttle.

Highland Classic Limousine and Shuttle
Raleigh / 919-231-6900

The limousines from Charlotte's Riches and Roses aren't flashy and don't have bedrooms, but the company has won awards for professionalism and, true to its name, every lady gets a free rose.

Riches and Roses Limousine Service
Charlotte / 704-637-1368

Finally, if you got really romantic about nine months ago, Diamond Limousine Service in Fayetteville suggests you take advantage of their newborn baby pickup service.

Diamond Limousine Service
Fayetteville / 910-630-1220

If a horse-drawn carriage is your idea of romantic, Springbrook Farms will pick you up at your Wilmington hotel, take you on a tour of downtown historic Wilmington, then drop you off at your restaurant of choice for dinner. They also have a special Valentine's Day package with a half-hour ride in an enclosed French evening coach with a box of flowers and a red rose.

Springbrook Farms, Inc.
Wilmington / 910-251-8889

Needless to say, all of these services will be happy to transport your wedding party in style!

Let's
Spend
the Night
Together

The deep joy we take in the company of people with whom we have just recently fallen in love is undisguisable.—John Cheever

In every romantic relationship, there will come a time when one of you pops the magic question: "So, do you want to go away for the weekend?" Overnight trips are a great way to advance or recharge a relationship. And while we didn't set out to write a guidebook to North Carolina's many, many hotels, resorts, and inns, we do want to leave you with some suggested getaways for romantic weekend (or longer) trips.

We've chosen a handful of spots in a variety of settings, from the coast to the mountains and from rural to urban. Most of these lodgings are near attractions we've featured elsewhere in the book, and some of them, especially the sports resorts, provide all the adventure you could want without ever leaving the grounds.

North Carolina boasts several hundred bed and breakfasts and thousands of hotels. Our intent here is to give you just an idea of the range of wonderful places to stay. Please see the appendix for additional sources of lodging information.

ONE OF A KIND

North Carolina may have lots of bed and breakfasts (many listed below), but we believe it has just one *boat* and breakfast, operated by Winds of Carolina Sailing Charters. Take a moonlight or sunset cruise out of Southport on the *Stephania,* a 37-foot sailing yacht. When you return to the marina, you'll spend the night alone on the boat, and the owners will bring you breakfast on board the next morning. If you want to add a bit of nightlife to your stay, you'll be docked near a small oak grove park with an open air Tiki bar and a dance floor. What a great idea for an anniversary or even a honeymoon!

Winds of Carolina Sailing Charters
Southport / 910-278-7249

COUNTRY INNS AND BED AND BREAKFASTS

For romantic overnights, many people gravitate toward country inns or bed and breakfasts because of the cozy atmosphere and often picturesque settings. We've chosen inns with a little bit of something for everyone, whether it's luxury, solitude, or scenery. Some have all the modern conveniences, but we've noted a few that eschew phone and/or television for true privacy. Rates range from affordable to expensive and often change seasonally; if your budget is tight, go off-season and get the extra bonus of smaller crowds. Most of these establishments serve breakfast and some also offer other meals.

Built in 1790, Baird House is a colonial-style inn set on 16 rolling acres adjoining the Watauga River near Valle Crucis. Although skiing, hiking, golfing, fishing, and rafting are convenient, and Grandfather Mountain and Linville Falls are close by, you can also just sit in a rocker on the front porch or share a hammock under an apple tree and watch the world go by.

Baird House
1451 Watauga River Road / Sugar Grove
828-297-4055 or 800-297-1342 / www.bairdhouse.com

Many of our informants recommended a stay at the Balsam Mountain Inn, an elegant restored inn that is on the National

Register of Historic Places. The fifty rooms are decorated in period style, and while each has its own bath, they've removed the distractions of televisions and phones. There's plenty to do nearby, including an excursion on the Great Smoky Mountain Railway or hiking or fishing in the crisp mountain air (the kitchen will prepare a picnic lunch for you, too). On a rainy day you can grab a book, puzzle, or game from the library and curl up in front of a lobby fireplace.

🌲 **Balsam Mountain Inn**
US Highway 23/74 / Balsam / 828-456-9498 or 800-224-9498
www.aksi.net/~cmark/balsam.htm

Ocracoke Island, accessible only by ferry, offers seclusion and small-town charm that is missing from some of the more bustling beach towns. Ocracoke's Berkley Manor has just twelve rooms, each with a Caribbean theme; Antigua has a two-person hot tub and private porch; St. Martin offers a fireplace and great view; Martinique is the most private, also with a two-person hot tub. The sunset views from the four-story tower are not to be missed.

🔦 **Berkley Manor**
NC Highway 12 / Ocracoke Island / 252-928-5911 or
800-832-1223 / www.berkleymanor.com

In historic downtown Edenton, the Captain's Quarters Inn offers special weekend packages for golfers, sailors, and mystery lovers. If you choose the mystery weekend, the two of you will team up to search for clues among the antique shops, historic buildings, and restaurants nearby. Whether or not you choose a special weekend package, the bedchamber of choice for romantics is The Captain of Her Heart Room, with a whirlpool for two and satin sheets.

🔦 **Captain's Quarters Inn**
202 West Queen Street / Edenton / 800-482-8945
www.captainsquartersinn.com

If you want to treat your true love like royalty, try a few nights at the Castle Inn on English Knob. You don't have to cross a moat to get to this turreted edifice, but you'll climb to 3,000 feet and be rewarded with stunning views of the Blue Ridge Mountains in every direction. You'll want to stay in the Royal Tower Suite, with a fireplace, whirlpool, and your own private observation tower. The elegant dining room serves breakfast, dinner, and afternoon tea.

Castle Inn on English Knob
Castle Way / Spruce Pine / 828-765-0000 or 800-925-2645
www.castle-inn.com

For pure privacy, you can't beat a night or two at the Charles Street Garden Suite in the mountain town of Saluda. Note that this establishment calls itself a suite, not an inn or hotel. That means that you get the place to yourselves! In addition to the bedroom, the suite includes a sitting and dining area, a small kitchen, and a private swing in the outside garden. It's a popular honeymoon spot and a convenient one too—an Episcopal church is right next door.

Charles Street Garden Suite
76 Charles Street / Saluda / 828-749-5846
www.members.aol.com/chasstgdn

One of the state's best-known inns, and deservedly so, the lovely Fearrington House is a AAA Five-Diamond winner for both lodging and dining. The rooms and suites are all decorated with antiques, fresh flowers, and original artwork. You can spend time strolling Fearrington Village's shops or travel to nearby Pittsboro for an afternoon of antiquing. Jordan Lake, with fishing, boating, and eagle watching, is also close at hand. The restaurant at Fearrington House, which we feature in our "Feeding Your Love" chapter, is outstanding.

Fearrington House
2000 Fearrington Village Center / Pittsboro / 919-542-2121
www.innbook.com/fearring.html

Nature lovers and privacy hounds will want a few nights at the Harborlight Guest House Bed and Breakfast in Cape Carteret. Each waterfront suite has a private entrance and a view of the Bogue Sound or Intracoastal Waterway (some have whirlpools and fireplaces). Suite 7 is not cheap, but it has a private deck, a gas fireplace, and views of the waterway from the two-person whirlpool. From your room or from a rocking chair on the porch, you might get a glimpse of porpoises or river otters feeding in the water.

Harborlight Guest House
332 Live Oak Drive / Cape Carteret / 800-624-VIEW (8439)
www.bbonline.com/nc/harborlight/

We really love the Inn at Celebrity Dairy, and so do visitors from all over the east coast who are drawn to its rustic country setting. Celebrity Dairy is a working farm that provides goat cheese to area restaurants and groceries; your country breakfast will include eggs gathered from the chickens that very morning. Each room, named for one of the resident goats, is decorated with whimsical hand-painted furniture and antiques; you'll find a robe in your wardrobe and bottled water on the nightstand. Nearby attractions include the North Carolina Zoo and the potteries at Seagrove, but you might just want to hang out on the porch or watch the milking at the "Goat Hilton" next door.

Inn at Celebrity Dairy
2106 Mount Vernon-Hickory Mountain Road / Siler City
919-742-5176 / www.celebritydairy.com

The Lodge on Lake Lure will remind you of those bygone days when entire families spent the summer at the lake house. Life might not be quite so carefree now, but try to grab a long weekend together at this rustic lodge on the mountain lake that *National Geographic* described as one of the ten most spectacular human-made lakes in the world. For some quiet time together, take one of the lodge's canoes or pontoon boats out for a spin; nearby attractions include Chimney Rock, the Blue Ridge Parkway, and the Brevard Music Festival.

Lodge on Lake Lure
Charlotte Drive / Lake Lure / 828-624-2789 or 800-733-2785
www.lodgeonlakelure.com

In a historic district near downtown Durham, Morehead Manor is a stately colonial home with four stunningly decorated rooms including a honeymoon suite. The owners, who are among the few African American bed and breakfast operators in the country, will greet you with a glass of wine and descriptions of nearby attractions, which include the Durham Bulls Athletic Park, just two blocks away, and Duke Gardens, a five-minute drive from the inn. With the Getaway Package, you'll get flowers and a sparkling beverage of your choice in the room, and in warm months, there is often jazz on the lawn.

Morehead Manor Bed & Breakfast
914 Vickers Avenue / Durham / 919-687-4366 or 888-437-6333
www.citysearch.com/rdu/moreheadmanor

If you love Victorian houses, you'll love Raleigh's Oakwood Inn. Situated in Raleigh's Historic Oakwood neighborhood, it offers old-fashioned charm along with modern conveniences like phones and televisions. For romance, we suggest the Polk Room with a private porch and queen-sized bed. In the afternoon, your hosts will serve fresh brownies or a glass of wine. If you want to venture out, go to the North Carolina Museum of Art or just wander around the neighborhood and look at the historic homes nearby.

Oakwood Inn
411 North Bloodworth Street / Raleigh / 919-832-9712 or
800-267-9712 / members.aol.com/oakwoodbb

If you always wanted to own a small mountain cabin together, but don't want to worry about maintenance and upkeep, an attractive alternative is a few nights at Pilot Knob Inn. Nestled in the foothills north of Winston-Salem, this inn features individual cabins with stone fireplaces, loft bedrooms, and whirlpools built for two. You can get out and explore nearby Pilot Mountain State Park or just stay on the grounds and indulge in the two-person dry sauna or wander over to the six-acre lake to hang out on the island gazebo.

Pilot Knob Inn
New Pilot Knob Lane / Pilot Mountain / 336-325-2502

Bald Head Island is not a desert island, but it might be the next best thing: an island without automobiles. You can enjoy this tranquil setting in one of the ten guest rooms at Theodosia's Bed and Breakfast. To get around the island, the folks at Theodosia's will let you borrow a golf cart or bike. Use them to explore the island's beaches, tidal creeks, and salt marshes, to visit Old Baldy, the island's historic lighthouse, or to head over to the Bald Head Island Club for a few hours of golf, tennis, or croquet.

Theodosia's Bed and Breakfast
Bald Head Island / 910-457-6563 or 800-656-1812
www.theodosias.com

Roanoke Island's White Doe Inn is a Queen Anne-style house located in the village of Manteo. Your room is furnished with all the necessities for a romantic sojourn: a fireplace, a CD player with a supply of romantic discs, Godiva chocolates, and a queen-sized bed. Surprise your sweetheart by asking for the Romantic Interludes package and you'll find champagne, cheese and crackers, and flowers in the room. If you want to come up for air, Cape Hatteras National Seashore is just five minutes away, or you could explore Manteo's Elizabethan Gardens or take hang-gliding lessons at Jockey's Ridge.

White Doe Inn
319 Sir Walter Raleigh Street / Manteo / 257-473-9851 or
800-473-6091 / www.whitedoeinn.com

UPSCALE LODGING

We like bed and breakfasts, but sometimes there's a blessed anonymity about staying in a large hotel, too. Here we highlight a few of the best, most luxurious hotels in the state. Attention to service is a hallmark of these places, and you will be pampered as much as you want at these establishments, most of which offer in-room meals, concierge services, and exercise facilities. You may want to check your credit rating before checking in—luxury hotel rooms come at a high price!

The smallest of the hotels in this category but definitely luxury class, Darlings by the Sea is ideal for busy couples who want to leave it all behind—but not too far behind. Luxury suites include a whirlpool for two, robes, satellite TV, in-room movies, and fresh flowers. Every suite has a private terrace overlooking the sea. Your gourmet breakfast is stocked in your room bar the night before, so you never have to leave your room. If you must check back with work or home, you have two separate phone lines and three telephones, including a portable that you can take to the beach!

Darlings by the Sea
329 Atlantic Avenue / Kure Beach / 910-458-8887 or
800-383-8111 / www.darlingsbythesea.com

Once a residential hotel and home to many of Charlotte's prominent citizens, the Dunhill Hotel is a small luxury inn that is listed on the National Register of Historic Places. On weekend afternoons, you can enjoy afternoon tea accompanied by live piano music at the Dunhill's Monticello Restaurant. Nearby is the North Carolina Blumenthal Performing Arts Center, and for more distant excursions, book a ride in the hotel's chauffeured stretch limousine.

Dunhill Hotel
237 North Tryon Street / Charlotte / 704-332-4141 or
800-354-4141

Probably the state's most famous hotel, the Grove Park Inn and Resort has been receiving guests from all over the world since 1913. With its spectacular views of the Blue Ridge Mountains and impeccable hospitality, this is a terrific getaway for couples. You don't have to leave the Inn to take in a meal at the award-winning Horizons restaurant, head to Elaine's for a night of dancing, or sip a nightcap in front of the fireplace at the Great Hall Bar. New in 2000 will be a spa with massage, whirlpools, and body and skin treatments. The many special packages offered by the Inn include the Marry Here package, which includes a magistrate, witnesses, a photographer, a bridal bouquet, and a wedding cake for two.

Grove Park Inn and Resort
290 Macon Avenue / Asheville / 828-252-2711 or 800-438-5800
www.groveparkinn.com

Built in the style of an Italian Palazzo, Fayetteville's Radisson Prince Charles Hotel combines period furnishings with modern amenities, from in-room bars to exercise facilities. The Executive Club Floor was designed for business travelers, but the privacy and luxury it offers should also appeal to couples wanting to get away from it all. Guests can take an old-fashioned horse-drawn carriage ride around historic downtown Fayetteville—perhaps on the way to or from their wedding!

Radisson Prince Charles Hotel
450 Hay Street / Fayetteville / 910-433-4444 or 800-678-8946

Many of the Sanderling Inn Resort's rooms offer an ocean or sound view, and every guest has access to the nearby white sands that make the Outer Banks so popular. Each room comes with plush robes, a private porch, and a wet bar or kitchenette. If just swimming or sunbathing isn't enough, the folks at the Inn will arrange a tee time or guided kayak tour or nature walk. Be sure to save time to watch the sun set!

Sanderling Inn Resort
141 Duck Road / Duck / 800-701-4111
www.outer-banks.com/sanderling

RESORTS FOR SPORTS

Our friends Lee and Tom, great sports fans, spent their honeymoon at a resort playing golf and tennis. If you, too, would like to plan a vacation around sports activities, these resorts are tailor-made for you. Once again, space permits us to list just a few such establishments, and we've chosen those that seem particularly suited for romantic sojourns.

Pinehurst Hotel and Country Club is the *crème de la crème,* the holy grail for golfers. Golfing on one of the resort's eight courses, you will follow in the footsteps of Jack Nicklaus and Arnold Palmer. To take a breather from golf, try one of the 24 tennis courts or the croquet lawn. Because of the pleasant climate, year-round play at each of these sports is a distinct possibility.

Pinehurst Hotel and Country Club
Village of Pinehurst / 800-IT'S-GOLF (487-4653)
www.PinehurstResort.com

At 3,600 feet in the Blue Ridge Mountains, the High Hampton Inn and Country Club provides a beautiful setting for golf. If your golf isn't going well, you can claim that the scenery distracted you! Golfers love the eighth hole, which is played to an island green.

High Hampton Inn and Country Club
Highway 107 South / Cashiers / 828-743-2411

Equally scenic is golfing on the coast, with the bonus that you can get in a game most any time of the year. Many coastal hotels offer access to nearby golf courses, where you can test your skills against wind and where getting caught in a sand trap takes on a whole new meaning. For luxury accommodations and golf all in one package, we suggest Beau Rivage Plantation and Country Club just outside of Wilmington. Framed by the "beautiful shores" of the Cape Fear River and the Intracoastal Waterway, it is a picturesque setting for a championship course.

Beau Rivage Plantation and Country Club
6230 Carolina Beach Road / Wilmington
910-392-9021 or 800-628-7080

The Washington Duke Inn and Golf Club offers elegant rooms, an eighteen-hole course recently redesigned by Rees Jones, and the award-winning Fairview restaurant. Athletic types who aren't into golf will want to explore the 3.2-mile jogging/walking trail that meanders around the golf course through a pine forest, particularly the separate fitness loop with exercise stations placed at 20-foot intervals. The Inn's Rendezvous Package includes golf-view accommodations, champagne and strawberries upon arrival, and other amenities.

Washington Duke Inn and Golf Club
3001 Cameron Boulevard / Durham
919-490-0999 or 800-443-3853
www.washingtondukeinn.com

For tennis buffs and equestrians, we can recommend the Inn at Yonahlossee, located adjacent to the Moses H. Cone Memorial Park near Blowing Rock and Boone. During your stay at either the lodge-style inn or adjacent private cottages, you can take advantage of the Yonahlossee Resort and Club's indoor and outdoor courts and equestrian facilities. Brush up on your tennis skills with private lessons from one of the Club's two pros. The Inn offers a popular Romantic Getaway Package several times a year.

Inn at Yonahlossee and Yonahlossee Resort and Club
226 Oakley Green / Boone / 828-963-6400 or 800-962-1986
www.yonahlossee.com

Experienced or novice horseback riders should book a stay at the Cataloochee Ranch in Maggie Valley, where you can explore the nearby mountain forests on full- or half-day guided trail rides. Longer backcountry trips can also be arranged, and the ranch also offers tennis, horseshoes, and croquet. Nearby is the Cataloochee Ski Area.

Cataloochee Ranch
119 Ranch Drive / Maggie Valley / 828-926-1401 or
800-868-1401 / www.cataloochee-ranch.com

Appendix: Further Resources

BOOKS

North Carolina Traveler: A Vacationer's Guide to the Mountains, Piedmont, and Coast, edited by Sunny Smith and Ginny Turner. Fifth Edition. John F. Blair Publisher. 1999.

North Carolina, by Sheila Turnage. Compass American Guides. 1998.

North Carolina: A Guide to Backcountry Travel and Adventure, by James Bannon. Out There Press. 1996.

Touring the Western North Carolina Backroads, by Carolyn Sakowski. John F. Blair Publishers. 1996.

North Carolina Beaches, by Glenn Morris. Revised and Updated Edition. University of North Carolina Press. 1998.

PERIODICALS

Our State: Down Home in North Carolina
800-948-1409
This monthly magazine is a great source for learning about places and happenings in North Carolina.

The RoMantic Newsletter
888-4ROMANTIC (476-6268)
www.theromantic.com
Produced by "the world's most romantic man," this newsletter is packed
with tips (mostly geared to men) on how to be more romantic. And it's
based in North Carolina!

ORGANIZATIONS

North Carolina Division of Tourism, Film and Sports Development
301 North Wilmington Street
Raleigh, NC 27601-2825
919-733-4171, 800-VISITNC (847-4862)
www.visitnc.com

North Carolina Association of Convention and Visitor Bureaus
1235-E East Boulevard, #213
Charlotte, NC 28203
704-333-8445
visit.nc.org
This organization's website includes links to all local and regional convention and visitor's bureaus.

North Carolina Division of Parks and Recreation
P.O. Box 27687
Raleigh, NC 27611-7687
919-733-7275

North Carolina Bed & Breakfasts and Inns
P.O. Box 1077
Asheville, NC 28802
800-849-5322
www.bbonline.com/nc/ncbbi

Carolina Mornings Bed and Breakfast Reservation Service
109 Circadian Way
Chapel Hill, NC 27516
800-770-9055 or 888-667-6467
www.carolinamornings.com
Tell them what sort of B&B you'd like to stay in and where, and they'll
book your room.

Carolina Culture Tours
1821 Hillandale Road, Suite 1B-120
Durham, NC 27705
919-416-0788 or 888-286-6272
www.culturetours.com
Tours that explore the arts and heritage of North Carolina, from day
trips to week-long adventures.

Index

Ackland Art Museum 18
Aeronautics 42
Albemarle 102
Albemarle Sound 81
Amazing Maize Maze 83
American Dance Festival 8
Amtrak 51
Andrews 56
Andy Griffith Show 28
Apex 30, 97
Appalachian Cultural
    Museum 18
Appalachian Ski Mountain
    54
Appalachian State
    University 6, 18
Appalachian Trail 54
Artifacts 78
ArtsCenter 5
Artspace 77
Ashe County Cheese
    Company 99
Asheboro 33, 72
Asheville 13, 45, 58, 66,
    76-77, 86-87, 98, 101,
    104-105, 116, 118, 133
Asheville Tourists 66
Asheville Wine Market 104
Atlantic Coast Conference 64
Ava Gardner Museum 17
Avon 51
Baird House 126

Bald Head Island 38, 131
Balsam 11, 127
Balsam Mountain Inn 11,
    127
Bank of America Queen's
    Cup 67
Barbecue Festival 108
Barnes & Noble 119
Basnight's Lone Cedar Café
    92
Beau Rivage Plantation and
    Country Club 135
Beaufort 88, 92, 95
Beaufort House Restaurant
    92
Beech Mountain 54
Belmont 12
Belmont Drive-In Theatre 12
Bennett Vineyards 102
Berkley Manor 127
BFDC 59
"Bikes on Board" 51
Biltmore Estate 57, 76-77
Biltmore Estate Winery 101
Biltmore Village 76-77
Black Mountain 78
Black Mountain Artist's
    Studio Tour 76
Blowing Rock 34, 53
Blue Ridge Ballroom 116
Blue Ridge Cycling
    Adventures 52

Blue Ridge Mountains 10,
    13, 128, 133, 135
Blue Ridge Parkway 43-45,
    130
Blue Ridge Rafting 55
Blythe Landing 31
Boat and Breakfast 125
Boating 55
Bodie Island Lighthouse 38
Bogue Sound 129
Books-a-Million 119
Boone 6, 18, 136
Border's 119
Brevard 10, 35
Brevard Music Festival 10,
    130
Bridal Veil Falls 36
Bright Leaf Drive In Theatre
    12
Bristol Books 119
Brookhill Steeplechase 68
Bryson City 27, 40, 55
Bull Durham 10, 13, 66
Bull Durham Blues Festival
    10
Bunker Hill Covered Bridge
    33
Burlington 32, 42, 66, 85
Burlington Carousel
    Festival 85
Burlington City Park 85
Burlington Indians 66

Burnsville 45
Butner 59
Buxton 39, 53
Buxton Stables 53
Cabbages & Kings 98
Calvary Episcopal Church and Churchyard 88
Canton 35, 40, 94
Canton Papertown Association 35
Cape Carteret 129
Cape Fear Botanical Garden 83
Cape Fear Crocs 65
Cape Fear River 79, 95, 135
Cape Hatteras Lighthouse 38
Cape Hatteras National Seashore 28, 131
Cape Lookout Lighthouse 39
Cape Lookout National Seashore 39
Captain's Quarters Inn 127
Carolina Ballet 8
Carolina Dancesport 116
Carolina Diamonds 67
Carolina Hurricanes 68
Carolina Mudcats 67
Carolina Panthers 68
Carrboro 5
Cary 21, 70
Cashiers 33, 37, 135
Castle Inn on English Knob 128
Castle McCulloch 40
Cataloochee Ranch 136
Chadler's Wharf 79
Chapel Hill 6, 14, 18, 65, 83, 93, 100
Charles Street Garden Suite 128
Charlie Goodnight's Comedy Club 114
Charlotte 4, 15, 20, 65, 68, 77, 84, 94, 105, 114-115, 120, 133

Charlotte Hornets 68
Charlotte Knights 67
Charlotte Regional Farmers Market 105
Charlotte Steeplechase 69
Charlotte Sting 68
Chelseas and the Village Tea Room 77
Cherokee 27, 53, 114
Chimney Rock 130
Chimney Rock Park 36
City Center Arts Gallery Walk 76
City Lights Bookstore and Café 118
City Market (Raleigh) 77
City Market (Winston-Salem) 78
Claremont 33
Clayton 69
Clemmons 53, 83
Clyde 41
Coker Arboretum 83
Cold Mountain 35
Colfax 105
College Sports 64
Comedy Club, Ramada Inn 114
Comedy Clubs 114
Comedy Zone 114
Continuing Education, Duke University 104
Cornelius 31, 115
Corolla 16, 39, 51
Cotton Exchange 78
Craft Heritage Trails 27
Craggy Gardens 44
Craggy Pinnacle 44
Crowders Mountain 29
Crystal Queen 95
Cucalorus Film Festival 13
Cullowhee 19, 65
Currituck Beach Lighthouse 39
Dare County Tourism Bureau 51

Darlings by the Sea 132
Davidson 6
Davidson College 6
Davidson Gallery Crawl 77
Dee Gee's Gifts and Books 119
Dennis Vineyards 102
Diamond Limousine Service 120
Diggs Gallery 18
Dillsboro 56, 96
Dirty Dancing 13
DoubleTake Film Festival 13
Dry Falls 36
Duck 51, 80, 93, 134
Duke Gardens 85
Duke University 6-7, 19, 64, 85, 104
Duke University Blue Devils 65
Duke University Museum of Art 19
Dunhill Hotel 133
Duplin Wine Cellars 102
Durham 6-8, 10, 12, 19, 57, 65-67, 85, 94, 104, 107, 115-117, 119, 130, 136
Durham Athletic Park 10, 66
Durham Bulls 13, 66
Durham Bulls Athletic Park 130
Durham Dragons 67
East Carolina University 6
East Carolina University Pirates 65
Eastern Music Festival 9
Edenton 81, 127
Edward 102
Elizabeth City 14, 119
Elizabeth City State University Planetarium 14
Elizabeth's Café and Winery 93

Elizabethan Gardens 84
Eno River Wafting 57
Fantasy Limousines 120
Farmers markets 104
Fayetteville 83, 114, 116, 120, 134
Fearrington House 93, 128
Fearrington Village 119
First Friday Gallery Walk 77
Flat Rock 7
Flat Rock Playhouse 7
Fletcher 110
Folk Art Center 45
Fort Mill 67
Frazier, Charles 33, 118
Fred Astaire Dance Studios 115
French Broad River 53-54
Gallery Row 78
Gastonia 67
Gatesville 28
Geldof Chocolatier 99
Germanton Art Gallery and Winery 102
Glass Onion Gourmet Market 97
Gourmet Garden Herb Farm 106
Governor's Walk 80
Grandfather Mountain 45
Graveyard of the Atlantic 26
Great Smoky Mountains National Park 27
Great Smoky Mountains Railway 54, 97
Greensboro 9, 19, 67, 80, 81, 85, 94, 107, 114-115, 120
Greensboro Arboetum 85
Greensboro Bats 67
Greenville 6, 65, 70
Grove Park Inn 133
Hammocks Beach State Park 29

Harborlight Guest House Bed and Breakfast 129
Harkers Island 39
Harrah's Cherokee Casino 114
Hatteras 106
Hatteras Village Aqua Farm 106
Henderson 12
Hendersonville 34, 81, 87
Henrietta II 95
Hickory 67, 102
Hickory Crawdads 67
Hickory Nut Falls 36
Hickory Nut Gorge 36
High Hampton Inn and Country Club 135
High Point 7
Highland Classic Limousine and Shuttle 120
Highlands 33, 36
Hospice League Balloon Festival 42
Hot Springs 55-56
Hot Springs Spa and Campground 56
Huntersville 31
Hurricanes University 68
Il Palio 93
Inn at Celebrity Dairy 129
Inn at Yonahlossee 136
Jamestown 40
Jazzy Ladies 20
Jetton Park 31
Jimmy V Celebrity Golf Classic 70
Jockey's Ridge 59, 132
Jordan Lake 30
Joyce Kilmer Memorial Forest 27
Jump Off Rock 34
Kannapolis 67
Kayaking 29, 53-56
Kill Devil Hills 32, 114
Kindred Spirits Mailbox 35
Kings Mountain 29
Kinston 67

Kinston Indians 67
Kitty Hawk 42
Kitty Hawk Aero Tours 42
Kitty Hawk Air Services 41
Kitty Hawk Kites 42, 59
Knotts Island 101
Know 118
Kure Beach 132
Lake James State Park 32
Lake Lure 13, 36, 96, 130
Lake Lure Tours 96
Lake Macintosh 32
Lake Mattamuskeet 30
Lake Norman 31
Lake Norman Yacht Charters 31
Lan's Gourmet Food, Gifts, and Cooking School 107
Last of the Mohicans 13, 36
Latta Plantation Nature Preserve 31
Laurey's Catering/Gourmet-to-Go 98
Lewisville 101
Lexington 108
Linville 45
Linville Falls 126
Lodge on Lake Lure 130
Lodgings 126
Looking Glass Falls 37
Love in the Tropics 18
Lumberton 19
Maggie Valley 136
Malaprop's Bookstore and Café 118
Manor House Bed and Breakfast Inn 51
Manteo 28, 51, 84, 98, 118, 132
Manteo Booksellers 118
Martin Vineyards 101
Masonboro Island 56
Mattamuskeet National Wildlife Refuge 30
Mattye Reed African Heritage Center 19

McIntyre's Fine Books and
Bookends 119
Merchants Millpond State
Park 28
MerleFest 11
Michael Jordan Celebrity
Golf Classic 70
Mile High Swinging Bridge
42
Minor League Baseball 66
Mint Museum of Art 15
Mint Museum of Craft +
Design 15
Moore Square Arts District
77
Mooresville 31
Morehead City 59, 119
Morehead Manor Bed &
Breakfast 130
Morehead Planetarium 14
Moses H. Cone Memorial
Park 136
Mount Airy 12, 98
Mount Mitchell State Park
45
Mountain Heritage Center 19
Museum of Anthropology 19
Museum of Early Southern
Decorative Arts 82
Nags Head 38, 42, 49, 51,
58, 59, 78, 92
Nags Head Woods Preserve
32
Nana's 94
Nantahala Gorge 56
Nantahala Gorge Ruby
Mine 40
Nantahala Outdoor Center
55
Nantahala River 55
National Black Theatre
Festival 8
National Park Service 26
Native American Resource
Center 19
Nebo 32

New Bern 16, 80
New Bern Heritage Tour 80
New Morning Gallery 77
North Carolina A&T
University 19
North Carolina Arboretum
86
North Carolina Azalea
Festival 86
North Carolina Black
Repertory Company 8
North Carolina Blumenthal
Performing Arts Center 4
North Carolina Botanical
Garden 83
North Carolina Department
of Transportation 50
North Carolina Division of
Parks and Recreation 26
North Carolina Farmers
Market 105
North Carolina Grape
Council 102
North Carolina Jazz Festival
10
North Carolina Mountain
State Fair 110
North Carolina Museum of
Art 15, 20
North Carolina Museum of
Natural Sciences 17
North Carolina Oyster
Festival 108
North Carolina Pottery
Center 16
North Carolina School of
the Arts 5
North Carolina Shakespeare
Festival 7
North Carolina State Fair 110
North Carolina State
University 6
North Carolina State
University Wolfpack 65
North Carolina Symphony
9

North Carolina Waldensian
102
North Carolina Zoological
Park 72
Oakdale Cemetery
(Hendersonville) 87
Oakdale Cemetery
(Wilmington) 88
Oakwood Inn 130
Ocean Atlantic Rentals 51
Ocracoke 27, 57, 127
Old Baldy 38, 131
Old Burying Ground 88
Old Pressley Sapphire Mine
40
Old Salem 82
Olympus Dive Center 59
Outer Banks 27, 38-39, 56,
80, 127, 134
Owens, "River" Dave, 57
Page After Page Bookstore
119
Paisley Pineapple 94
Pamlico Sound 55
Panthertown Valley 37
Pewter Rose Bistro 94
Picnics 97
Picnics to Go 98
Piedmont Boll Weevils 67
Piedmont Triad Farmers
Market 105
Pilot Knob Inn 131
Pilot Mountain 28, 131
Pinehurst 86, 135
Pinehurst Hotel and
Country Club 135
Pineville 115
Pinnacle 28
Pisgah Covered Bridge 33
Pisgah National Forest 35
Pittsboro 56, 93, 119, 128
Point Fermin Lighthouse
78
Pullen Park 85
Quail Ridge Books 118
Queens Landing 31

Radisson Prince Charles Hotel 133
Raft 'n' Rail 56
Raleigh 6, 8-9, 15, 18, 20, 26, 37, 50, 65, 67-68, 77, 85, 99, 103, 105, 110, 114-116, 118, 120, 130
Raleigh Jaycees 69
Raleigh Road Outdoor Theatre 12
Raleigh Wings 67
Ramsey Creek Park 31
Reds Beach Music 116
Reed Gold Mine 40
Regulator Bookshop 117
Replacements, Ltd. 80
Resorts for sports 134
Reynolda House 15
Riches and Roses Limousine Service 120
Ride the Wind Surf and Kayak 57
Riverside Cemetery 87
Riverwalk 79
Roanoke Island 131
Roanoke River 56
Robbinsville 27
Rock Rest Adventures 56
Rogallo Kite Festival 42
Roland's Dance Studio 116
Roosters Gourmet Market and Gifts 107
Rose Hill 102
Salisbury 50
Saluda 128
Sanderling Inn Resort 133
Sandhills Horticultural Gardens 86
Scarborough Faire 80
Schoolhouse Falls 37
Sea Scan Dive Centre 58
Seaboard Wine Warehouse 103
Seagrove 16
Shallotte 107

Siena Hotel 93
Siler City 129
Silohouse Vineyard and Winery 102
Sixth and Trade Art District 78
Ski Beech Ski Resort 54
Smithfield 17
Smokemont Riding Stables 53
Songwriters in the Round 11
SourWood Grille at Springdale Country Club 94
Southern Season 100
Southern Waterways 57
Southport 126
Springbrook Farms 121
Springdale Country Club 94
Spruce Pine 128
Stanfield 40
State Street Station 81
Sugar Grove 126
Summerfest 21
Sunset Beach 35
Swan Quarter 30
Swansboro 29
Sylva 118
Tanglewood Park 52
Tanglewood Steeplechase 53
Tarboro 88
Teensy Winery 102
Thalian Hall 5
Theodosia's Bed and Breakfast 131
Tryon Palace 16
Twilight Dinner Train 96
Union Mills 102
University of North Carolina at Chapel Hill 6, 18, 64
University of North Carolina at Charlotte 85
University of North Carolina at Charlotte 49ers 65

University of North Carolina at Pembroke 19
University of North Carolina Tar Heels 65
University of North Caroliona at Greensboro 19
Valdese 102
Valle Crucis 126
Vantage Golf Tournament 50
Villar Vintners of Valdese 102
Wake Forest University 19
Wake Forest University Demon Deacons 65
Washington Duke Inn and Golf Club 136
Waterrock Knob 44
Waynesville 13, 52, 78, 102
Waynesville Drive In Theater 13
Weatherspoon Art Gallery 19
Weaverville 106
West Jefferson 99
West Point on the Eno 57
Westbend Vineyards 101
Western Carolina University 19, 65
Western Carolina University Catamounts 65
Western North Carolina Farmers Market 105
Whalehead Club 16
White Doe Inn 132
Whiteside Mountain 33
Whitewater Falls 37
Wilkesboro 11
Wilmington 5, 10, 13, 41, 79, 82, 86, 88, 95, 103, 115, 119, 121, 135
WindDancers Llama Treks 41
Winds of Carolina Sailing Charters 126

Wineseller 103
Winkler Bakery 82
Winston-Salem 5, 8, 15,
    18-19, 67, 78, 115, 131
Winston-Salem State
    University 18
Winston-Salem Warthogs 67
Yadkin River 28
Zebulon 67